CONCISE
LINCOLN
LIBRARY

—

EDITED BY RICHARD W. ETULAIN,

SARA VAUGHN GABBARD, AND

SYLVIA FRANK RODRIGUE

GREGORY A. BORCHARD

Abraham Lincoln and Horace Greeley

Southern Illinois University Press
Carbondale

Southern Illinois University Press
www.siupress.com

Copyright © 2011, 2019 by the Board of Trustees,
Southern Illinois University
All rights reserved. Cloth edition 2011.
Paperback edition 2019
Printed in the United States of America

22 21 20 19   4 3 2 1

The Concise Lincoln Library has been made possible
in part through a generous donation by the Leland E.
and LaRita R. Boren Trust.

Cover illustration adapted from a painting by Wendy
Allen

ISBN 978-0-8093-3046-1

The Library of Congress has cataloged the hardcover
edition as follows:
Borchard, Gregory A.
Abraham Lincoln and Horace Greeley / Gregory A.
Borchard.
       p. cm.— (Concise Lincoln library)
Includes bibliographical references and index.
ISBN-13: 978-0-8093-3045-4 (cloth : alk. paper)
ISBN-10: 0-8093-3045-8 (cloth : alk. paper)
ISBN-13: 978-0-8093-9065-6 (ebook)
ISBN-10: 0-8093-9065-5 (ebook)
1. Lincoln, Abraham, 1809–1865. 2. Greeley, Horace,
1811–1872. 3. Presidents—United States—Biography.
4. Politicians—United States—Biography. 5. Journal-
ists—United States—Biography. 6. Newspaper edi-
tors—United States—Biography. 7. United States—
Politics and goveßrnment—1861–1865. I. Title.
E457.2.B68 2011
973.7092'2—dc22
[B]   2011003166

Printed on recycled paper ♻

For Horace Greeley's great-great-great-grandson Theodore Horace Greeley Dake, who by chance or fortune in 2005 took my History of Journalism class at the University of Nevada, Las Vegas, and later allowed me to peruse his family album, providing literal evidence that history not only lives but also makes itself known to us in the most unexpected ways

CONTENTS

Preface   ix

Introduction: Abraham Lincoln and Horace Greeley
     Remembered   1
1 Self-Made Men   5
2 Thirtieth Congressmen   27
3 Free Soil, Free Labor, Free Speech, Free Men   44
4 A Fight for Union and for Freedom   67
   Conclusion: Re-remembering Lincoln and Greeley   90

Notes on Sources   105
Notes   115
Selected Bibliography   127
Index   133

Gallery of illustrations following page 43

PREFACE

Writing about either Abraham Lincoln or Horace Greeley should humble any historian, as nearly every account of their lives recognizes them as extraordinary Americans. When given the opportunity to write about both of them, I was also reminded of an observation from Edwin Emery, an honored media historian, who noted that few people in the Civil War era come close to Lincoln in being the subject of study, but Greeley is one of them.[1] United by their beliefs in the American System—a model of nationalism promoted by influential Whig statesman Henry Clay—as well as in Clay's celebration of "self-made" careers that contributed to American society, Lincoln and Greeley combined remarkable political and journalistic talents to create legacies much larger than those of ordinary men.

What follows is a profile of the professional relationship between Abraham Lincoln, on his rise to the presidency, and his most famous counterpart in the press, Horace Greeley, editor of the influential *New York Tribune*. It expands on individual biographies of the men by weaving discussion of their short congressional terms together with a retelling of their roles in the Civil War. It suggests a dialectical relationship between Lincoln's role as a politician and Greeley's role in the press, one that combined Lincoln's conservative belief in a social order with a myriad of progressive policies published in Greeley's *Tribune*, including the promotion of free soil in the West, a government devoted to national infrastructure development, and an eventual end to slavery.

While a number of histories recognize the important roles held by Lincoln and Greeley during the Civil War, few (if any) have detailed the development of their relationship during the 1840s and 1850s. Traditionally, an understanding of Lincoln's legacy has focused primarily on written accounts from his presidency, but in recent years, archivists have discovered previously neglected artifacts that shed new light on his story. Archivists have identified Lincoln, for example, in photos of the Gettysburg Address that they previously assumed showed no sign of him. Likewise, with Greeley's story, new technologies, including the digitization of nineteenth-century newspapers—including none other than Greeley's monumental *New York Tribune*—have allowed for the revisitation of otherwise decaying newspaper sources with a greater precision, speed, and ease in searching for key people, places, and events. As a result, the stories of Lincoln's life and Greeley's life remain as complex and deserving of study today as they did more than a century ago.

In writing this monograph, as both a historical and a journalistic endeavor, I sought to interpret what other sources have written about Lincoln and Greeley by gathering facts and arranging them into a narrative about the events that shaped their lives. I hope readers will find the resulting account as compelling as its subjects: two figures who should not be studied separately—and who, it will be seen, were not entirely "self-made"—with stories as challenging as the subject of American history itself.

I would like to thank Michael Green, who helped make this work possible, and S. J. Barlament, an exceptional copy editor who helped proof drafts of chapters along the way. Readers directly affiliated with this project deserve special recognition for their attention both to detail and to the overall meaning of this work: Dick Etulain, who provided insight and advice on integrating Lincoln sources; Sylvia Frank Rodrigue for her suggestions on tuning and clarifying content; and Sara Gabbard, who helped review statements for accuracy. Friends and colleagues David Bulla and Elaine Parsons provided feedback on contextual items, including historical events and personalities that deserved recognition in this text. Thanks also go to Paul Traudt, who in hosting an archival trip to Germany in 2008 helped provide an international perspective on the subjects of this book. I have also been fortunate to have the help of students at the University of Nevada, Las Vegas, including Kenthea Fogenay, Amanda Laken, Ji Hoon (Jay) Lee, and Christine Powell, who transcribed copies of Greeley's handwritten letters and articles from the *New York Tribune*, the *Chicago Tribune*, and the *New York Times*. I especially appreciate the support of Ardyth Sohn, director of the Hank Greenspun School of Journalism and Media Studies, who recognized that historical studies, although time consuming, deserve scholarly attention.

ABRAHAM LINCOLN AND HORACE GREELEY

INTRODUCTION: ABRAHAM LINCOLN
AND HORACE GREELEY REMEMBERED

In an event wrongly relegated to a footnote, Abraham Lincoln and Horace Greeley both visited Chicago for the first time in July 1847, meeting for a political rally that helped secure their careers of national importance in both politics and the press. Organizers had originally promoted the Chicago River and Harbor Convention as a protest of President James K. Polk's veto of a bill that would have invested federal funds into Chicago, a city of rising importance in the West.[1] Although neither Lincoln nor Greeley at the time considered the moment pivotal, it would go on to secure their roles on the national stage, foreshadowing a reconvergence of national leadership in Chicago during the 1860 Republican convention.

When the news of Polk's decision had reached Chicago, ships there lowered flags to half-mast, demonstrating that many in Illinois believed Polk's action would be a crippling blow against an otherwise developing economy. Responding to the crisis, the convention attracted a veritable "who's who" of leading Whig and Democratic politicians and editors. Among delegates, Schuyler Colfax, editor of Indiana's *St. Joseph Valley Register*, headed the list of secretaries in charge of the event. Other attendees included Lincoln, a rising Whig just beginning a term in the U.S. House; Greeley, the popular editor of the *New York Tribune*; David Dudley Field, famed reformist lawyer; and Edward Bates, the presiding officer who in 1861 would become attorney general in Lincoln's cabinet. Leading national political figures—Henry Clay, Martin Van Buren, and Lewis Cass—read letters, gave addresses, and developed resolutions, adopted unanimously, calling on Congress to fund the construction of canals and railroads. With more than 10,000 conventioneers supporting calls to appropriate money for infrastructural improvements throughout the West, Lincoln spoke briefly, praising the attendees for their unity.[2] Greeley, describing for readers the event, noted his roles as both a participant and a reporter, introducing Lincoln to readers as "a tall specimen of an Illinoisan, just elected to Congress from the only Whig district in the State."[3] Although Lincoln's name had previously appeared in Greeley's newspaper as a notation of his election to the House, this was apparently the first time the Illinoisan had directly captured the attention of his editorial match in the East.

Newspapers in Lincoln's home state of Illinois described his contributions with even greater attention, assuring readers that they could trust him, their newly elected legislator in the U.S. House. "We expect much from him as a representative in Congress," reflected the *Chicago Journal*, "and we have no doubt our expectations will be more than realized, for never was reliance placed in a nobler heart and a sounder judgment."[4] Greeley, who on the day of adjournment, July 7, 1847, served as the committee chair to adopt a resolution calling for the construction of a railroad between Chicago and the Pacific, also showed promise as a politically minded reformer, noting that the "the cause of Internal Improvement, with the subsequent growth of Chicago, received considerable impetus from the Convention."[5] When Ohio Whig Thomas Corwin closed the meeting and addressed the delegates by issuing a call for the *Tribune* editor, Greeley rose to the occasion. He spoke to an attentive audience about the need for federal investments in the West and was "warmly cheered," according to Thurlow Weed, Greeley's mentor also in attendance. For the first time, Greeley emerged for serious consideration as a political candidate.[6]

The event was one of many in which the careers of Lincoln and Greeley intersected. Their shared belief in the United States united them, personified in their mutual admiration for Henry Clay, who had described his model for the Union as the American System—a collection of regions bound by a government that advanced the interests of both the regions and the whole. As fellow Whig representatives, one from Illinois and—with Greeley's election in 1848—the other from New York, the two men formally began working together, in accordance with these shared beliefs, in the Thirtieth Congress. While Lincoln's outspoken criticism of the Polk administration's prosecution of the Mexican-American War defined his legislative term and Greeley's service was remarkable for his advocacy of public rights to lands in the West, both worked toward the eventual end of slavery.

Having grown to adulthood under similar circumstances and each having developed a sense of self-reliance at an early age, the two men lived through the nation's severest test, the Civil War, and gave subsequent generations direction in understanding both America's past and its future. Indeed, this self-reliance—or as Clay, one of the most influential statesmen of the nineteenth century, had described it, their living representations of the "Self-Made Man"—characterized both their individual experiences and those they shared.[7]

Their professional careers, by necessity, separated the two men, with Lincoln's life determined primarily by the political and legal climate of the mid-nineteenth century. During the first part of his career, Lincoln maintained generally moderate positions and, his biographers tend to agree, expressed a conservative temperament, believing as a young man that the role of his generation was to transmit the values of the nation's Founders. But, over time, Lincoln came to believe that each generation would need to redefine America in relation to the current problems it faced, and, by the middle of the Civil War, he would declare, "The dogmas of the quiet past are inadequate to the stormy present." In the final few years of his life, he began thinking in the future tense, saying, "We must think anew and act anew."[8] Lincoln's life, in many ways—especially during this transformative time—would therefore serve as an appropriate representation of not only the men and women of his era but also Americans both before and after the Civil War.

The press-based legacy of Greeley's career, meanwhile, included his admirable attempts to publish—for a substantial portion of the nineteenth century—a variety of perspectives on the extraordinarily critical issues of the day. Greeley's critics pointed to the seemingly endless variety of reforms favored by the editor as evidence of an erratic, if not unstable, personality; along with pressing for women's rights, the emancipation of slaves, and the end of the death penalty, the *Tribune* advocated causes including temperance, vegetarianism, socialism, communitarianism, spiritualism, and utopianism. But these same "isms," the supporting of which Greeley's critics perceived as a fundamentally irrational editorial approach, in the end made him one of the most remarkable moral leaders of his day, as his passion to see justice done, whether or not it was popular, gave him the courage to write on behalf of the dispossessed and disenfranchised. Only after his death did many who criticized him come to recognize his unstoppable character as a virtue. Having lost the presidential election of 1872 to incumbent president Ulysses S. Grant and broken by the physical and mental toll of the campaign, he died shortly thereafter, at the age of sixty-one. When he was buried on December 4, 1872, critics who had made sport of him and admirers alike mourned the loss of the nation's best-known editor, a memory of him that lives to the present day.[9]

With the continuing popularity of their individual stories saying much about those who have followed them, the lives of Lincoln and Greeley have touched readers for more than 150 years. While these men shared endeavors and worked separately on others, agreeing on some policies while disagreeing on others—just as individual members of subsequent generations have—they, in doing so, personified the complexities, virtues, contradictions, and faults of their eras. Speaking and writing to us as they spoke and wrote to their fellow Americans years ago, with each audience member at the time and each historian in years that followed interpreting them differently, each man will continue to have an audience as long as readers and writers find their words an indelible part of our shared lives.

SELF-MADE MEN

While the lives of Abraham Lincoln and Horace Greeley generally followed parallel paths, those paths intersected at times, leaving the two men legacies both distinct and interrelated. They shared similar origins and made a natural match in their respective careers of politics and the press. In their early lives, they became loyal followers of the Whig Party and its most outspoken leader, Henry Clay—a bond that provided the intersection for their evolutions. Although the first known direct contact between Lincoln and Greeley—at least the first in which they formally worked together—came in December 1848, when they served in the Thirtieth Congress, they had shared interests in campaigns well before their respective debuts as legislators. While Lincoln followed the content of the widely popular *New York Tribune*, as did most midwesterners, Greeley, the newspaper's editor, advocated the political policies favored by Lincoln and his constituents in Illinois. And although they lived hundreds of miles from each other and saw each other only on rare occasions, both advocated essentially the same political policies, distinguishing themselves as the leading disciples of Clay. Where the two men disagreed, mostly, was on how best to achieve their goals.

Both of the Lincoln and Greeley families came to America (as had many of their generation) during the time of Charles I and Cromwell, with Lincoln's ancestor Samuel Lincoln, a weaver, leaving Hingham, England, and Greeley's ancestor Andrew Greele (the surname was not spelled Greeley until the third generation in America), a miller, leaving Nottingham. Samuel settled in Hingham and Andrew in Salisbury, both in Massachusetts. Both families migrated (the Lincolns to New Jersey, Pennsylvania, Virginia, and Kentucky and the Greeleys to New Hampshire, Vermont, and Pennsylvania) and raised large numbers of children; family members became weavers, millers, blacksmiths, ironmongers, carpenters, and farmers—mainly jobs that required a level of self-sufficiency, hard work, and independence. Neither family had members who were college-educated, and both Abraham and Horace were for the most part self-taught, learning what they needed for their respective careers through voracious reading on their own time. These traits suited each to work naturally within a nineteenth-century philosophical perspective on life that held that human society generally worked on benevolent terms, gradually progressing with each new generation, and that under these conditions, individuals could work to improve themselves. These ideas, which later became associated with a "Whig" vision of history (one that cast humanity on a constant move toward progress), were not necessarily synonymous with the Whig Party of the nineteenth century, but one of the party leaders, Henry Clay, did contribute largely to a vision shared by followers of a national, harmonious system based in Whig policies.

Henry Clay, a Kentuckian of the same hardscrabble background as Lincoln and Greeley, devoted his life to politics and, in seeking both mass appeal and the betterment of the nation, developed a reputation as the "Great Compromiser." Although he received three nominations for the presidency in his four decades of service, he never won the office that his supporters so earnestly sought for him. As Speaker of the House and the Democratic-Republican candidate, Clay lost to John Quincy Adams in the controversial election of 1824. In 1832, when Clay ran again (and lost again, this time as the National Republican candidate), both Lincoln and Greeley, in the first presidential election in which the two men were eligible to vote, cast their ballots for him. Over the next year, the National Republicans collapsed, and a new party, the Whigs, replaced them, adopting at least a few old ideas, including many that Clay had advocated. In Clay's final nomination for the presidency, as a Whig in the stunningly close election of 1844, he again lost, but only after Lincoln, Greeley, and almost half of all voters gave him their support.

Clay's political ideals included a form of nationalism he dubbed the American System, an organization of state and local governments tied by a federal system that linked manufacturing in the Northeast with grain production in the West and the cotton and tobacco crops of the South—a vast, interdependent economic web greater than its parts. The key to the success of this model included individual contributions from a particular kind of citizen, whom Clay had described (in helping to coin the phrase) as "self-made."[1] In using the phrase, Clay had most likely been referring to the types of business entrepreneurs with whom he had associated in Kentucky. While Lincoln, who shared Kentucky roots, in later years illustrated the concept of self-improvement, the notion itself became an ingrained part of the American psyche only through Greeley and other Whigs—and, later, through Horatio Alger's rags-to-riches myth—who popularized the idea. From their earliest days as aspiring professionals to their final days at the end of their respective careers, Lincoln and Greeley were guided by these Whiggish notions of self-improvement and self reliance—this "self-madeness"— which determined their legacies in a way they had both, to a certain extent, created.

Lincoln in the Age of Clay

Historians may appropriately describe the early lives of Lincoln and Greeley relative to the presidency of Andrew Jackson (1829–37)—so influential that the antebellum era has been described as the "Age of Jackson"—as more accurately part of the "Age of Clay."[2] Henry Clay, the primary opponent of Jackson's Democratic Party, in fact shared a commensurate role in both the trajectory of the nation at the time and the careers of his most notable followers. Rooted in a system that celebrated "the common man" (as did Jackson's Democrats), Lincoln, Greeley, and Whigs in general sought to expand Jefferson's vision for the United States beyond the spoils of partisan loyalty by accentuating individual endeavors with the helpful hand of a republican government dedicated to national interests.

Accounts of Lincoln's early life typify the mythology of the Age of Clay, with various sources—including one written by Lincoln himself—retelling the rearing of the future president in a log cabin. In February 1860, he reflected in an autobiography, "I was born Feb. 12, 1809, in Hardin County, Kentucky. My parents were both born in Virginia, of undistinguished families—second families, perhaps I should say." About his lack of a formal education, he described the frontier area as "a wild region, with many bears and other wild animals, still in the woods," in which he received little schooling beyond "readin,' writin,' and cipherin' to the Rule of Three."[3] Other details about Lincoln's boyhood years stem from his own characterization of them as the "annals of the poor."[4] He remembered his father left the Knob Creek area of Kentucky for land free of slavery, for reasons both economic and religious. His most formative experiences took place in his new family home in Indiana, a recently admitted state. Young Abraham's first years there consisted of intense work for his father to help clear a settlement area, including room for one of the rustic log cabins that later brought him fame.

In his early twenties, Lincoln set out on his own to work on a river flatboat. He then moved to New Salem, Illinois, and, working as a clerk and surveyor, began his interest in politics. He launched his political career in March 1832 with the announcement of his candidacy for the Illinois General Assembly. From April to July 1832, he served as a volunteer in an Illinois militia unit during the Black Hawk War, and although he saw no fighting—later joking that he only had "a good many bloody struggles with the *mosquitoes*"—he was promoted to captain, having demonstrated leadership capabilities.[5] Lincoln's campaign for the fall election, revolving primarily around the undertaking of navigational improvements for the Sangamon River, was unsuccessful, but on his second try for public office, voters elected him to the Illinois legislature in 1834. Soon thereafter, he earned a state law license and moved to Springfield, where he began a law partnership and won reelection to the legislature in 1836, 1838, and 1840. At the age of thirty-three, he married Mary Todd, a well-to-do Kentuckian, and nine months later, their first child, Robert, was born. At thirty-seven, he was elected to the U.S. House for one term. In 1849, ten years before Oregon's statehood, he declined a patronage offer to become its territorial governor, allowing his political life to quiet until the mid-1850s, when, in the midst of sectional strife that was tearing at the nation, he reemerged as a national candidate. Accepting the nomination to run against Stephen A. Douglas for the U.S. Senate, he declared famously, "A house divided against itself cannot stand."[6]

While the backdrop for the widely known Lincoln-Douglas debates had taken decades to develop—with the press playing a crucial role in the formation of the American political experience—the foundation upon which both Lincoln and Greeley built their careers can be understood only through the lens of what historians have described as the First Party System. Before Lincoln's and Greeley's debuts as national figures, parties had stemmed from divisions between those who favored the powers of state governments (advocated by Thomas Jefferson) and those who supported a strong national government (advocated by Alexander Hamilton). By the mid-1830s, a new form of partisanship replaced the Anti-Federalist/Federalist Parties, birthing the Second Party System of American political organization.

Although voters of the era recognized the importance of party affiliation, the names of parties alone tell only part of the story of the evolution in American politics. While Democrats of the 1830s and 1840s shared the party name traditionally associated with Jefferson, their opponents, the Whigs, would claim to advocate more consistently the rights of individuals that Jefferson had sought to protect. Indeed, in later years, after receiving an invitation to attend a birthday commemoration for Jefferson, Lincoln suggested it was the Whig Party, and then the Republicans, that had maintained the Founder's vision for the United States. "It is both curious and interesting that those supposed to descend politically from the party opposed to Jefferson, should now be celebrating his birthday," he wrote. The Democrats of the 1850s, he continued, "hold the liberty of one man to be absolutely nothing, when in conflict with another man's right of property. Republicans, on the contrary, are for both the man and the dollar; but in cases of conflict, the man before the dollar."[7]

The complexities of the system that had emerged in the 1830s included campaigns for local and national offices, along with recognizably modern techniques (many of which are still popular today) that included wide use of the media to reach an increasingly democratized electorate. Martin Van Buren, who became the eighth president, first pioneered the art of creating an image for a candidate in 1828, working from the top of the Democratic Party down. On behalf of his mentor, Andrew Jackson, Van Buren drew primarily on state leaders such as Thomas Hart Benton of Missouri and on urban leaders such as Alan Campbell of Louisville to construct a national political organization and determine issues of importance to the electorate. The campaign worked, using popular themes such as Jackson's heroic performance in war—his strength as a commander, like the durable wood used to make various campaign items commemorating him, earned him the moniker "Old Hickory"—and in the next election, the same techniques would contribute to Van Buren's own election to the presidency.

Such campaign innovations set the tone for politics and the press for following decades—indeed for subsequent American history—and techniques were developed for both those aspiring to elected office and those promoting them in the press. The new political affiliations consisted of Democrats and Whigs, with members of the former finding roots in the Jefferson/Jackson party line and members of the latter finding their base in a federation of state and local organizations and expressing outrage over Andrew Jackson's "Caesarism," or his alleged contempt for the separation of powers and the rule of law. While Jeffersonian Democrats had maintained that deviations in mental and physical capabilities among men were not great enough to account for differences in wealth distribution, Whig campaigns promoted the tariff and the reformation of laws that had worked, since even before the Revolution, to keep the ownership of land and property in the hands of a wealthy ruling class.

During the Jackson and Van Buren administrations, the number of participating voters had more than tripled. At the same time, the ascent of the Whigs from obscurity to challenging the Democratic machinery appealed to voters otherwise disenfranchised in an age of populism—an age that Jackson, one of the most admired and, at the same time, hated presidents in history, had fueled. Jackson's

Democratic Party promoted liberty for the common man, but those to enjoy the spoils of the Democratic machinery did not include slaves, women, Native Americans, or, for that matter, Whigs. The resulting split in American society along partisan lines developed an extraordinary and combustible political mix that fueled both the best and, in some cases, the ugliest features of the American experience.

The pride shared by Lincoln and Greeley in the United States was strengthened by a belief in a government based upon the will of the people and in their natural rights—a nationalism that combined Revolutionary American ideas with a belief in the benevolence of society and Union. Clay had advocated this kind of nationalism in his idea of the American System, advancing particular Whig economic and trade policies. But while Lincoln, Greeley, and Clay were likeminded in their advocacy of a national bank, Lincoln focused, in his early career, on issues of special interest to his constituents in Illinois, including infrastructural improvements in transportation that would help the development of local commerce.[8]

Clay, Lincoln, and Greeley shared another important belief—the eventual end of slavery—and worked toward achieving that goal. Clay, however, unlike Lincoln and Greeley, had himself owned slaves, making his position problematic, though not entirely atypical. While Clay could claim in the abstract to represent the legal rights both of slaveholders as well as of those who opposed slavery on moral grounds, he could not in political terms represent the nation as a whole, which had by increments grown irreconcilably divided over the issue. In addressing the question over whether Americans could continue to own humans, Lincoln and Greeley, through speeches and editorials, each answered with an unambiguous "no."

While Lincoln was still among the youngest members of the Illinois legislature, the opportunity to address slavery thrust itself upon him both unexpectedly and violently. In November 1837, a proslavery mob attacked and killed Elijah Parish Lovejoy in Alton, Illinois, after the Presbyterian minister had attempted to begin publishing an abolitionist newspaper. Shocked at the murder, Lincoln was among the few to speak publicly about it. In a January 27, 1838, address before the Young Men's Lyceum in Springfield, Lincoln condemned the Illinoisans behind the act. "The innocent, those who have ever set their faces against violations of law in every shape, alike with the guilty, fall victims to the ravages of mob law," he said. "Let every man remember that to violate the law, is to trample on the blood of his father, and to tear the charter of his own, and his children's liberty."[9] On various occasions leading up to his fateful campaign for president—during his term in the U.S. House, after the passage of the Kansas-Nebraska Act, and certainly during his debates with Stephen A. Douglas in the 1858 campaign for Senate—Lincoln repeatedly spoke against slavery in ways that Clay could not, seeking to end the institution.

Greeley, who would emerge as one of the nation's leading antislavery editors, held a connection to the events surrounding Lincoln's career in Illinois through a longstanding belief that the West—where he believed free labor alone should be allowed to flourish—was the solution to the physical, economic, political, and spiritual conditions ailing the urban centers of the Northeast. And as Lincoln's early years in politics as a member of the Illinois legislature revolved around the issues of land speculation, bank regulation, and the construction of canals and railroads—all of which grew directly from the expanding American frontier—Greeley, too, played a part in the West's economic growth. Believing free access to public lands in the West would produce "the ultimate emancipation of labor from thralldom and misery," Greeley called for the chance for each man to earn the fruits of his labor, reasoning that the protection of lands in the West provided the working class this opportunity.[10]

At first, Greeley had reserved his comments on slavery to editorials on its economic backwardness, avoiding the issue as a decidedly unfruitful one in regard to attracting readers. But the *Tribune*'s tone changed noticeably when it became clear that President Polk had waged the Mexican-American War to extend the territorial reach of the United States and consequently to enable slavery to continue to thrive. The late 1840s thus marked Greeley's arrival as an outspoken opponent of the institution, visible in his attacks on it as not only economically regressive but also a social abomination and moral sin. For Greeley, slavery also represented a fundamental reason to remove the Democratic Party from power. "When we find the Union on the brink of a most unjust and rapacious war," he wrote in response to Polk's attack upon Mexico, "then we do not see how it can longer be rationally disputed that the North has much, very much, to do with Slavery. If we may be drawn in to fight for it, it would be hard indeed that we should not be allowed to talk of it."[11]

Like Lincoln, Greeley held a lifelong record of opposing slavery, but—also like Lincoln—his attitude toward African Americans reflected racist notions that had permeated American society, North and South. Despite Greeley's famous call for abolition, which he published in 1862 under the title "The Prayer of Twenty Millions," a *Tribune* editorial printed in 1860 revealed a more calculated, if not cynical, position on the issue. "We make no pretensions to special interest in or liking for the African Race," Greeley wrote. "We hope the day will come when the whole negro race in this country, being fully at liberty, will gradually, peacefully, freely, draw off and form a community by themselves."[12] Lincoln, too, had entertained the possibility of recolonization as a solution to the slavery issue before issuing the Emancipation Proclamation, as the idea of integrating slave laborers into the free society of the North commonly struck even the most progressive thinkers as impossible.

For Lincoln and Greeley, as well as for antislavery whites in the North in general, the issue of slavery resonated more clearly as an economic one than it did in racial terms. Lincoln and, no doubt, many of his midwestern counterparts played a distinct role in developing the national economy. While they generally supported federal policies that helped populate the frontier, they were also almost entirely responsible for creating their own livelihoods. Reflecting on a visit to Beardstown, Illinois, Lincoln described seeing a steamboat crew loading cargo onto the vessel, working, in his words, "like galley slaves and being cursed every moment by the brutal mate." The scene disgusted him, demonstrating as it did the "tyranny" of a system in which white men were the equivalent of chattel.[13]

This situation put both his father and himself at odds with the nation's developing political system. While Thomas Lincoln would naturally have supported the populist programs of President Jackson

—namely, those designed to extend the access to land among rural farmers—he also opposed on moral and religious grounds (as his son Abraham's autobiography noted) the same policies that allowed the extension of slavery. The social predicament that faced the Lincolns has led to some disagreement among historians as to whether Thomas Lincoln was a Whig or a follower of Jackson.

It is clear that Abraham Lincoln at an early age began reading the business-minded *Louisville Journal*, a newspaper with a strong anti-Jackson/pro-Clay editorial bias that no doubt fueled his interest in the Whig philosophy championing the entrepreneurial spirit. He used the newspaper as a political tool for the first time when he sought reelection to the Illinois state legislature. Having completed his first two-year term, the twenty-seven-year-old candidate living in the village of New Salem published a letter in the *Sangamon Journal* on June 18, 1836. "I go for all sharing the privileges of the government who assist in bearing its burdens," he wrote, making it known that he favored suffrage rights for all who paid their taxes, "by no means excluding females," a common political sentiment among members of the emergent Whig Party.[14] Lincoln's letter also expressed his support for Whig candidate Hugh L. White, who, along with William Henry Harrison (in his first bid for the presidency), ran on the first presidential ticket featuring Whig Party presidential nominees. Harrison finished a respectable second to Democrat Martin Van Buren, Andrew Jackson's appointed heir, carrying seven states for seventy-three electoral votes during the election later that fall.

The voters of Sangamon County sent seven men to the legislature in 1836 and made Lincoln the head of the delegation. Having been reelected to a second term, Lincoln enjoyed a role of importance as Whig floor leader, and the *Sangamon Journal* began publishing his speeches, the first appearing in January 1837. At nearly the same time, Lincoln earned his law license, and the Illinois legislature chose Springfield as its permanent capital. Beginning practice in an office next door to the *Journal*, he became accustomed to visiting the editors and talking politics. In the following years, Lincoln practiced politics and law, developing a reputation as one of Illinois's leading Whigs, a distinction he carried during his successful bid for Congress.

Greeley had also called for universal emancipation since his earliest days as a struggling printer, and by the time of the 1860 presidential election, the imagery of the log cabin—first popularized by Greeley himself in his 1840 *Log Cabin* newspaper—represented the freedom that he saw the West as offering for all people: men and women, white and black. Indeed, Greeley's *Tribune* of 1860 was among the chief promoters of Lincoln's biography, explaining in stories and transcriptions of popular stump speeches how the successful Illinois lawyer had grown up in poverty in "the very humblest White stratum of society" and how he had earned his own livelihood by "the rudest and least recompensed labor."[15] These renditions no doubt resonated with Greeley, who at the age of fifteen had left his impoverished home to make a life for himself as a writer. Lincoln—a true frontiersman, the *Tribune* noted—cleared primeval forests, split rails, ran a flatboat, and worked his way gradually upward to knowledge, influence, and competence. In his early life, Lincoln had helped support his family and at the same time had educated himself, reading by firelight in the family log cabin—another bond he shared with Greeley, who had also developed a reputation as an avid reader and self-taught stylist.

The Radical Whig

Horace Greeley's sympathies for the working class stemmed, no doubt, from his own experiences and familial background. His father, Zaccheus Greeley, had married Mary Woodburn in 1807 and raised Horace, born February 3, 1811, in the farming town of Amherst, New Hampshire. In an odd passage from the classic *Life of Horace Greeley*, author James Parton describes Greeley's life as exceptionally full of struggle, right from the beginning: "The effort was almost too much for him . . . he came into the world as black as a chimney. . . . There were no signs of life. He uttered no cry; he made no motion; he did not breathe. But the little discolored stranger had articles to write, and was not permitted to escape his destiny."[16]

Zaccheus Greeley suffered economic hardship during the Panic of 1819, and although Horace received irregular schooling until age fifteen, he nonetheless developed a voracious appetite for reading. In 1826, he sought work as a young apprentice at the *Northern Spectator*, a weekly newspaper in rural East Poultney, Vermont. When the paper failed, he moved briefly to Erie County, Pennsylvania, and in August 1831, at the age of twenty, he gathered his possessions and traveled to New York City. Arriving with only ten dollars in his pocket, he worked as a newspaper compositor and found refuge in the meetings of Workingmen, a group organized to advocate the rights of laborers. In January 1833, Greeley and fellow worker Francis V. Story opened a printing office that began issuing the *Morning Post*; although short-lived, it was among the first of a new group of newspapers dubbed the penny press, which relied on cheap prices, sensational content, and low advertising rates to reach a large number of readers. He began his career as a political publisher the next year, founding the *New-Yorker*, a weekly literary and news journal featuring politics, social issues, and the arts and sciences, and in 1836, he married Mary ("Molly") Y. Cheney, a Connecticut schoolteacher whom he had met at a New York boardinghouse for Grahamites, a group devoted to healthy dietary practices.

Just as Greeley's publishing career had begun to emerge, the Panic of 1837 (an economic depression attributed to unregulated land specu-lation, bank failures, and a subsequent financial collapse) afflicted the nation. New York City suffered extraordinarily. The Whigs credited the collapse to Jackson's failure to provide financial confidence, which stemmed, they alleged, from his veto of the recharter for the national bank. Meanwhile, Greeley, surrounded by signs of extraordinary crisis, entertained radical ideas as a way to address economic chal-lenges directly. "The times were hard, fuel and food were dear," wrote biographer Parton, who was also one of Jackson's many biographers. Some of New York City's residents died of starvation and others froze to death during the unusually severe winter.[17]

Greeley was drawn specifically to Fourierism, a model of com-munal organization promoted by French socialist Charles Fourier, who, in reaction to the horrors he had witnessed during the French Revolution, developed the idea of an ideal regime of group organiza-tion he called "Harmony." In October 1841, the *Tribune* premiered a column by Albert Brisbane, an American disciple of Fourier's who had studied under the utopian in Paris. Brisbane—and in turn the

Tribune—advanced the doctrine that government should give each person the opportunity to select a vocation within a communal unit called a "phalanx," which consisted of 1,620 men working 5,000 acres of land. When Greeley compiled Brisbane's proposals and published them in book form in 1843, he earned scorn from critics who dubbed him "Horatius the Fourierite"; however, Brisbane had attracted followers who applied the theory to financial and social institutions.[18] *Tribune* readers appreciated the editor's concern for the dispossessed, and in 1844, after serving as first vice president of a Fourierite convention in New York, Greeley was toasted for having Americanized the cause. Responding to the *Tribune*'s calls for agricultural development, communes spread throughout the Northeast and Midwest in the 1840s and 1850s and into the 1860s. Although Greeley was successful in transforming the transcendentalist Brook Farm in Massachusetts into a Fourierite association, it—and other such communities—functioned for just a few years before organizational insufficiencies caused it to close. After consistent failure with his own endeavors to head associations, Greeley attributed his frustrations to the types of people drawn to the movement—"the conceited, the crotchety, the selfish, the headstrong, the pugnacious, the unappreciated, the played-out, the idle, and the good-for-nothing generally."[19]

Whigs, more generally, attempted to engineer revolutionary political campaigns, most notably for presidents throughout the 1840s. To do so, they co-opted many of the tools, devices, and tricks that Martin Van Buren had used in his campaigns for Jackson during the 1820s, utilizing the emergent mass media to energize the electorate and demand a change in executive administration. It was as a direct result of those efforts that Greeley first met Thurlow Weed, editor of the *Albany Evening Journal*. Greeley had achieved a level of popular recognition with the *New-Yorker*, which demonstrated his talents as a literary editor, and Weed, one of New York's most powerful insiders, took an interest in acquiring Greeley's services. The project was to be a new journal, the *Jeffersonian*, which would promote the gubernatorial campaign of Weed's friend William H. Seward, later a rival of Abraham Lincoln's for the 1860 Republican nomination. Greeley accepted the offer, for which Weed paid him a thousand-dollar salary, and began issuing the paper in February 1838, christening what was informally described as "The Firm of Seward, Weed, and Greeley" (or, depending on the source, Weed, Seward, and Greeley—or Greeley, Weed, and Seward).[20] Greeley filled the *Jeffersonian* with political news and congressional speeches, aiming to persuade readers with reasoned debate, rather than with the typical stories of crime and vice generally featured in the popular penny press newspapers of the time (such as the *New York Sun* and the *New York Herald*). The *Jeffersonian* was short-lived—in part because Seward's election made publication no longer necessary—but Greeley's connection with Weed would later help him launch the *Log Cabin*, a campaign weekly promoting the second presidential bid of William Henry Harrison.

The Log-Cabin Candidate

The Whig Illinois state convention met in October 1839 and chose Abraham Lincoln as a delegate for the national convention in Harrisburg, Pennsylvania. Along with more than 250 other delegates, Horace Greeley also attended, but he and Lincoln either did not notice each other or made no record of meeting each other. The Whig national convention adopted no official platform, and the Whigs' presidential candidate, General William Henry Harrison, expressed few views—though among them was that Congress should not abolish or interfere with slavery except upon the application of states, nor should it abolish slavery in the District of Columbia without the consent of its residents. But with his silence seeming to reinforce Democratic assertions that he was a simple "General Mum," Harrison broke with a tradition that held it beneath the dignity of candidates to speak on their own behalf by addressing a crowd in Columbus, Ohio, on June 6, 1840. It was the first of twenty-three speeches he delivered throughout that fall, ranging in length from one to three hours and refuting charges that he was incompetent and senile. The speeches and a harvest of souvenir items unsurpassed to this day in quantity and variety—from thread boxes and papier-mâché snuffboxes to flasks, cotton chintzes, bandanas, novelty medals, and tokens—marked 1840 as a watershed year in American politics, as both politicians and the electorate participated in innovative and unprecedented ways.

Lincoln's experience with the Harrison campaign was historic in another respect, pitting him against political rival Stephen A. Douglas, who would debate critical questions with him among the electorate in the following decades. Douglas, as head of the Democratic Party in Illinois, issued a challenge to Lincoln for a full-scale debate on the campaign issues. Lincoln accepted, and in the months leading to the convention, the two engaged in widely publicized discussions. From the accounts of Lincoln's contemporaries, his performance in the first set of debates did not meet even his own expectations.[21] He asked for another opportunity to state the case for the Whigs, and although he received the chance and later performed better, attendance at the second series of debates was small. Regardless, in both sets of debates, Lincoln emphasized key items on the Whig agenda, such as the need for a central bank and the promotion of growth among private businesses.

Lincoln's performances were extraordinary inasmuch as he was able to give rational and logical defenses of the Whig platform at a time when rallies replete with revelry and hard cider had more generally begun to sweep the electorate. One such event—an October 1840 Whig meeting in Rockford, Illinois—featured banners that bore slogans such as "Whigs of Byron—For Our Country We Rally" and "Pacatonic—No Tonic for Van Buren." With Harrison supporters lambasting President Van Buren as a "groveling demagogue" and dubbing him one of the "eastern officeholder pimps," Lincoln kept his composure.[22] He helped issue campaign literature, addressing it to local political committees, saying, "We have the numbers, and if properly organized and exerted, with the gallant Harrison at our head, we shall meet our foes and conquer them in all parts of the Union."[23] On Election Day 1840, Lincoln's fellow Illinoisans cast a majority of votes for Van Buren, but Lincoln himself had gained valuable long-term experience dabbling with the press, using part of his time campaigning to help prepare the Whig newspaper the *Old Soldier*.

Lincoln had reason for optimism, at least in the months that immediately preceded and followed what would become the first

Whig presidency. In a letter to John T. Stuart, whom he first met during the Black Hawk War and who was his law partner between 1837 and 1841, he expressed an energy common within the Whigs' popular movement. "I have never seen the prospects of our party so bright in these parts as they are now," he wrote. Noting that subscriptions for the *Old Soldier* had begun to "pour in without abatement," he believed confidently that the Whigs would "succeed triumphantly."[24]

The presidential election had pitted the incumbent Van Buren, supported by the beneficiaries of Jackson's affiliates, against a hungry party out of power. Harrison had earned a war-hero image as governor of Indiana when he defeated a confederacy of tribes headed by Native American leader Tecumseh and his brother, known as the Prophet, in a battle near the Tippecanoe River. Harrison was promoted under the slogan "Tippecanoe and Tyler, Too," a catchy Greeley creation that referred both to Harrison's victory and to his vice presidential running mate, John Tyler. The alliterative Greeley phrase became a small but effective part of the public's fascination with the Harrison campaign, an electoral spectacle that ironically had been sparked by a smear. The Van Burenite *Baltimore Republican*, in December 1839, had suggested that Harrison was too old for the presidency and that the best thing he could do for himself and for the country was to retire in a log cabin with a pension of two thousand dollars a year and a barrel of hard cider.[25] After other Democratic newspapers circulated the same innuendo, Whig editors spun the commentary as a slur by the eastern elite against the great American yeomanry, co-opting the reference and turning it on its head by promoting Harrison as "the Log-Cabin Candidate," a commoner who shared the folksy individualism of westerners, a large and growing demographic. An 1840 letter to Harrison from Governor Seward noted, for example, the establishment of Tippecanoe clubs and the erection of mock log cabins, promising a majority of 20,000 votes for the Whigs in New York alone.[26] Harrison did, in fact, own a log cabin in North Bend, Ohio—one built near the turn of the century, earning him the title "the farmer of North Bend"—but despite popular perception of his rustic image, he was an aristocrat, born not in a log cabin but in a fine two-story brick home on Virginia's James River.

As part of the overall mass-marketing campaign, the *Log Cabin* newspaper—another Greeley original—became the Whigs' major organ during the 1840 race. Subscribers ordered the newspaper until it was almost impossible to get clerical help fast enough to take care of the mail, and the first issue of 20,000 prints in May 1840 sold out at a rate greater than even Greeley could anticipate. The newspaper's success stemmed primarily from its tone—Greeley used an energetic style and an editorial voice that took pains not to insult the intelligence of his readers. The *Log Cabin* also engaged in a number of modern media practices, including the use of pre-election projections, to tantalize the audience. A chart of popular votes in the October 31, 1840, issue predicted Harrison would win the electoral college by a breakdown of 194 votes to Van Buren's 100. (Harrison won the election with 52.9 percent of the popular vote and popular returns very close to published projections but with a 243–60 majority and even more electoral votes than Greeley had projected.)[27] By the end of the campaign, the *Log Cabin* boasted a national circulation of 80,000 copies a week and a far-reaching influence that included the engagement of an audience energized to elect Harrison—compound feats that press historians have recognized as one of the most successful journalistic enterprises up to that time.[28]

Seward and Weed, Greeley's sponsors, quickly recognized Greeley's role in the Harrison campaign and encouraged him to build on his success. The result was the *New York Tribune*, essentially an attempt to reach Manhattan's working-class audience with a range of political content similar to that contained in the *Log Cabin*, from local and national news to the advocacy of Whig political ideas. In very real ways, this new newspaper more than any other of the antebellum era demonstrated an approach to publishing that respected readers, printing viewpoints from a broad cross-section of contributors—including women and other ordinarily marginalized members of society—with the simple prerequisite that their entries would build up and not tear down the *Tribune*'s audience.[29]

From a political standpoint, the publishing technique belied a political strategy as well. With New York's thirty-six electoral votes making the state essential for presidential candidates, Seward, Weed, and Greeley planned to advance their influence by capturing Manhattan's working-class audience, thereby securing their control over the state's governorship and, ultimately, over future presidencies. As Greeley had used Harrison's victory as the opportunity to dedicate the *Tribune* to act as an agent for social transformation, he made it a worker-based publication and, in the words of labor historian John R. Commons, "the first and only great instrument the country had known in the advancement of constructive democracy."[30]

Despite wide celebration of the Whig victory over the previous months, the March 1841 inauguration in intemperate weather exacted a final toll on Harrison.[31] On April 3, 1841, a small paragraph on page 2 of the *Log Cabin* disclosed discreetly that the president had taken ill with pneumonia. Within a week, Greeley reissued the newspaper with headlines announcing Harrison's death.[32] In historic irony, Greeley released the first issue of his subsequently famous *New York Tribune* on the day of Harrison's funeral, April 10, 1841, a day he described in his own words as a "leaden, funereal morning, the most inhospitable of the year."[33]

For the next thirty years, Greeley edited what would become the greatest single journalistic influence in the country. After attracting an original 500 subscribers by the end of its second month in circulation, Monday through Friday issues of the *Daily Tribune* had reached 11,000 newspapers each day, and by the end of the decade, the Saturday issue of the *Weekly Tribune*, especially popular in the Midwest, outsold all other newspapers in print.[34] The content of the *Weekly* in particular was alert, cheerful, and aggressive, and as he had done with the *Log Cabin*, Greeley drew readers with extensive coverage of issues that directly interested them, including farming reports and market prices as well as political campaigns and the endeavors of literary and intellectual figures. Hiring women as a way both to advance their careers and to lift the stature of his newspaper in enlightened circles, Greeley also promoted Margaret Fuller's feminist work in the *Tribune*, bringing her international fame as America's first female international correspondent.

Clay and the Dark Horse

A radical transformation had begun to take place in American society, epitomized by the introduction of Samuel F. B. Morse's telegraph, which, on May 25, 1844, with a series of magnetic dots and dashes, transmitted the words "What Hath God Wrought?" The machine on a basic level reinvented the way editors published news by making stories almost immediately available to readers. "Speed with Heed" became the new mantra of American journalism as a communication revolution took place, making the telegraph king. On a larger level, a nation of regional interests suddenly opened upon itself, a phenomenon described by historian Daniel W. Howe as giving a new urgency to social issues in general and to the controversy over slavery in particular.[35]

For both Lincoln and Greeley, the period marked a transformation in their careers that coincided with commensurate changes in American political communications. In the same year that Morse introduced the telegraph, Henry Clay's final campaign for president served as a demarcation point in the transformation of contests between Democrats and Whigs (and later Republicans) into regional competitions among increasingly nationally minded candidates. Whig idealism—an idealism that Clay had defined and was described by Lincoln as a role for government that did "for the people whatever needs to be done, but which they cannot, by individual effort, do at all, or do so well, for themselves"—gave way to practicality.[36] Greeley had also subscribed to the idea that government should not act merely as "a machine for making war," but the results of the 1844 election soured this vision, leading both Lincoln and Greeley to make unexpected compromises in their subsequent careers.[37]

With both Lincoln and Greeley having supported Clay their entire careers, Illinois again made Lincoln an elector for the Whig ticket in 1844, and Greeley again attended the Whig convention, held this time in Baltimore. With 40,000 attendees, the event was one of the largest political assemblies of the era. Clay—who had, since his days as Speaker of the House, acted as secretary of state from 1825 to 1829 under President John Quincy Adams and served as a Kentucky senator from 1831 to 1842—again entered the race for the presidency, initiating his campaign confidently with a written acceptance message read to the delegates by a spokesperson. His supporters resolved to adhere to a platform that called for a protective tariff providing revenue sufficient for the payment of federal debts, for the development of a uniform national currency, and for the allocation of lands in the West to free settlers—among the first calls for what would become the Homestead Act.

But, by the time of the 1844 election, political alliances had come to represent something more than allegiances to issues alone—they entailed deeply personal connections with individual personalities, which prior to Harrison had only begun to emerge as critical in swaying the electorate toward a particular party. Clay was a friend of the family of Lincoln's wife, Mary, and Lincoln had admired him as one of the ideal political leaders of the day. Likewise, Clay had inspired Greeley's interest in politics since well before the Harrison campaign—Greeley had in fact lobbied for Clay's nomination over Harrison's, but he counted himself, as did Lincoln, as a Whig first and foremost, agreeing to support the party nominee.

In the estimations of both Lincoln and Greeley, Clay's personality transcended Clay the individual, who by 1844 represented a way of thinking about the United States that could allow citizens to improve individual lives. In the months leading up to the election, Lincoln had changed course and, deciding to focus on his law career and his family, allowed the nomination for his place in the legislature to go to another Whig. He instead invested his political energies into speaking vigorously on Clay's behalf, addressing Clay clubs where party faithful met to sing songs praising "Gallant Harry" and to hear their hero's merits extolled. Lincoln had grown effective in his oratory, much more so than in his debates with Douglas in 1840—so much more so, in fact, that his contemporaries considered him the finest political speaker in the state of Illinois. For his part, Greeley campaigned and showed, in the words of biographer James Parton, "how hard a man can work, how little he can sleep, and yet live," risking his newspaper's credibility with a claim that the Whigs would carry New York by 20,000 votes.[38]

While both Lincoln and Greeley (as well as Whigs generally North and South) had in 1840 promoted the national bank, in 1844, regional differences began to split the party into distinct factions, first economically and eventually along lines of labor—primarily the free-labor and slaveholder axis. Lincoln and Greeley both supported the protective tariff as a way to combat the Democrats, who favored low customs duties and free trade. And, although the tariff issue by 1844 had lost favor with many Whigs, it continued to make recurring appearances in both Lincoln's stump speeches and Greeley's *Tribune* editorials.

When Clay accepted the role as front-runner for the Whig presidential nomination in 1844, his supporters had reason for hope. The central issue of the campaign regarded the annexation of Texas as a slaveholding territory, and both Clay and Democratic front-runner Martin Van Buren, who was looking to reclaim his spot in the White House, had published letters publicly declaring their opposition to the proposal. Both parties, with the nomination of their respective candidates, had expected to neutralize the slavery issue, which had become increasingly toxic for both those in office and those seeking office. However, pro-annexation Democrats, upset with Van Buren's silence on the matter, rejected him and chose instead a dark-horse candidate, James K. Polk—an expansionist from Tennessee—running him on a pro-annexation (and by default, a proslavery) platform.

The Clay campaign made a dramatic misstep in July, when a letter published in an Alabama newspaper, the *Tuscaloosa Independent Monitor*, inadvertently betrayed the understanding that Clay's supporters had of his stance on slavery. The letter suggested that Clay's objection to immediate annexation was not meant to please abolitionists, whom he denounced; instead, he stressed a concern for preserving the Union. The contents of the letter swayed enough voters who had been ambivalent supporters of Clay to switch their votes to Polk, simply because Clay had apparently vacillated on an important subject. The difference in votes ultimately proved significant enough to turn the election in critical areas, with the tallies revealing the closest presidential race of the era: Clay lost a crucial 2.3 percent of New York's vote to Liberty Party candidate James G. Birney, who had

62,263 votes nationally, leaving Polk with a plurality, not a majority, of the popular vote. Clay received 1,288,533 popular votes to Polk's 1,327,325, resulting in both candidates winning 48.1 percent of the vote. Polk, however, had managed to win 170 electoral votes to Clay's 105, with a difference of only 5,000 votes from New York separating Clay from the White House. Lincoln took Clay's defeat as a cue to redouble his efforts in seeking higher office—a seat in Congress—while Greeley, upon hearing the news, broke down in tears.

The defeat marked a critical turning point in the careers of both men—for Lincoln as an Illinois legislator and a lawyer and for Greeley as a popular New York publisher—leading both of them to congressional office and revealing to the nation both who they were and what the likely trajectories of their subsequent lives would be. Lincoln's contemporaries envisioned him as a rising star, part of a transformation during the era that saw the collapse of Whig opposition and the formation of the Republican Party. Greeley's contemporaries, meanwhile, appreciated his ability to write thoughtful editorials and reach an admiring audience that included erudite city dwellers, farmers, and homesteaders. In the Midwest, according to a famous description, settlers read Greeley's newspaper "next to the Bible."[39]

As Lincoln grew as a politician, seeking to preserve the Union amid regional strife with practical purpose, Greeley provided what he believed was the visionary idealism necessary to do so, advocating both a transcendental belief in harmony and a strong moral disdain for social transgression. Lincoln spoke primarily for free-soil interests and specifically for those of white farmers in the West and Greeley for those of labor and urban dwellers in the East. But the two men developed remarkably similar interpretations of nationalism (or what had previously been understood as the American System) at an extraordinary moment—a time during which their ideals collided with a peculiar and incompatible institution. The resulting conflict was one that neither Lincoln nor Greeley had anticipated, nor was it one that either man could adequately address during his lifetime; however, falling back on their shared beliefs in their defeated hero Henry Clay, they pressed forward toward higher office.

CHAPTER TWO

THIRTIETH CONGRESSMEN

The dark horse had won, dashing whatever hopes Abraham Lincoln and Horace Greeley had held for what proved to be Henry Clay's final presidential bid. President James K. Polk, seeking to extend the territorial reach of the United States across the continent, led the nation into a controversial war with Mexico (1846–48) over lands in the West. As debates in Congress and in the press focused on how the war would affect the extension of slavery, Lincoln's political career began receiving national exposure for his outspoken opposition, as a Whig legislator in Congress, to the war. Greeley, who emphasized slavery's evils in the *Tribune*, joined Lincoln for a short term in the House, advancing the interests of settlers in the West with proposed homestead legislation.

For a few fateful months in the late 1840s, Lincoln and Greeley shared in their service as Whig legislators, developing a trajectory for their collaborative efforts in the years to follow. After introducing resolutions that condemned the president's actions leading to the war, Lincoln finished his term and temporarily retreated from politics to focus on law, and Greeley reached new heights with his publishing record, influencing audiences on an international level.

Lincoln had, in 1842, stepped aside from the chance to run again for the Illinois state legislature and, as he would do at various times before his 1860 presidential campaign, shifted focus to his legal career. In 1843, he became a father when his wife, Mary, gave birth to their first son, Robert, whom Abraham referred to as his "dear

Bobby."[1] Developing his legal career, Abraham Lincoln's clients in law included railroad and insurance companies, merchants, manufacturers, and banks. He also worked on less glamorous legal matters, including patent suits, deeds, land registers, and taxes. But after the heart-wrenching Clay loss in 1844, and given the chance to refocus his energies in the following years, Lincoln reemerged as a political figure, this time as a candidate for the U.S. House after he secured the Whig nomination in 1846.

After a bout with depression due to the Clay loss (he described the condition as a "brain fever"), Greeley also refocused his energies and began using his social capital as the well-known head of the popular *Tribune* to promote his own interests. On several occasions, he broached the subject of political office to his sponsor, Thurlow Weed. "Should the Whigs of the legislature see fit to designate the two senatorial delegates," he wrote Weed, who as a powerful lobbyist could provide financial and political support, "I have a great mind to ask that my name be considered among the candidates for that honor."[2] Although Weed considered Greeley an important player in helping organize the party, he did not take seriously the editor's requests for political backing, as Greeley, who had demonstrated a talent for publishing, also alienated political and practically minded supporters with his constant (and sometimes contradictory) penchant for morals and "isms."

Meanwhile, a new generation of politicians and editors emerged, including Lincoln, his rival Stephen A. Douglas, and Joseph Medill and Dr. Charles Henry Ray—editors of the *Chicago Tribune*—threatening both the East's dominance over political affairs and the prominence of papers such as New York's *Herald* and *Tribune* over electoral issues. Although the Chicago newspaper advocated essentially the same political policies as Greeley's regarding western settlement, Medill and Ray were more in tune with the desires and needs of farmers and could sense more appropriately which candidates for office would best represent the West.

With eastern Whigs recognizing Chicago as a vital new hub, essential for the kinds of transportation and infrastructural developments encouraged by Clay's American System, western Whigs (and later Republicans, with Lincoln foremost among them) benefited directly in trade routes and commerce agreements from the strategy. And while the Northeast establishment, until the late-1850s, had the luxury of vacillating in its support of western candidates (with the *New York Tribune*, for example, suggesting that the victory of Stephen A. Douglas over Lincoln in the 1858 Senate campaign would benefit Republicans), the *Chicago Tribune*, first published in 1847, relentlessly supported Lincoln before and during his presidency.

Antiwar Whigs

Ten days after Lincoln's nomination for the House in the spring of 1846, the United States went to war against Mexico. The Polk administration called for 50,000 volunteers, and 300,000 answered. The *Sangamon Journal*, which supported Lincoln's campaign, demanded the president adopt a stern policy with Mexico for having allegedly spilled American blood on American soil. Lincoln's campaign speeches did the same, suggesting that the United States should maintain a hard-line policy with Mexico. The combination of press and speeches worked, securing Lincoln's election as a representative for Illinois's Seventh Congressional District. The area had always been a Whig stronghold—no Democrat had ever won the congressional seat in the district—but in 1846, Lincoln won by the largest margin for a Whig up to that time.

A month after Lincoln won his race for Congress, the Illinois legislature elected Congressman Stephen A. Douglas to the U.S. Senate, and by the time Lincoln made his appearance in Congress, almost a year later, the war with Mexico was in its final stages. Eyeing Douglas's Senate seat, Lincoln recognized the need to make his presence known and decided to use the war, which had grown increasingly unpopular, against the Democrats, writing in December 1847 to his law partner William Herndon, "As you are all so anxious for me to distinguish myself, I have concluded to do so before long."[3]

Historians have debated the exact reason for Lincoln's outspoken opposition to the war, as his motives must have included a mix of heartfelt belief and political maneuverings. He said he believed that whatever concerns there may have been about the constitutionality or necessity of the war, patriotic citizens should "remain silent on that point, at least until the war had ended." He also said he continued to hold that view until he took his seat in Congress and heard President Polk "argue every silent vote given for supplies, into an endorsement of the justice and wisdom of his conduct."[4] Regardless, two weeks after having written Herndon of his plans to "distinguish" himself, Lincoln introduced resolutions in the House that addressed eight questions to the president, demanding he tell the exact spot where Mexicans had shed American blood. He called for an explanation to the American people regarding "the spot of soil on which the blood of our citizens was shed" and for Polk to explain if this spot was on American land, as the president had alleged, or in fact within the territories of Spain.[5] Lincoln used the word "spot" three times in the address, which made his demands known as the "Spot Resolutions."

Lincoln resumed his attacks on the administration in January 1848, telling the House that he had examined all of the president's messages to see if Polk's assertions about precedents measured up to the truth. Before declaring war, the Polk administration had used the location of the first conflict with Mexico as the rationale for invading, claiming it took place on American soil. But the exact location of the initial conflict—near the border between Texas and Mexico and marked in part by the Nueces River—became itself the subject of controversy, as Lincoln alleged that it was not clear that the hostilities had actually taken place in the location claimed by Polk. "Now I propose to show," Lincoln said, "that the whole of this—issue and evidence—is, from the beginning to end, the sheerest deception." After analyzing six propositions of the president's evidence, Lincoln called on Polk to answer his charges with the same kind of honesty that later became associated with Lincoln himself: "Let him answer with facts, and not with arguments. Let him remember he sits where Washington sat, and so remembering, let him answer as Washington would answer."[6]

Lincoln's January speech to the House received support from a few Whig newspapers, but the response overall was critical. In Springfield, Illinois, the *Democratic State Register* typified the reception, editorializing that Lincoln's expressed opposition to the war was "little expected at the hands of his constituents, many of whom have been immortalized themselves by their gallantry and heroism in the bloody ravines of Buena Vista and rugged fastnesses of Cerro Gordo." The response of his fellow Whigs in Congress was to offer a resolution that tempered the criticism, first thanking General Zachary Taylor, a popular figure, for his role in the defeat of Santa Anna at Buena Vista, with a rider attached—the Ashmun Amendment, charging Polk had started the war unnecessarily and unconstitutionally. With Lincoln's support, the resolution passed by one vote, prompting the *State Register* to ask what the state's "gallant heroes" would think of their representative when they returned from Mexico.[7]

Lincoln continued to demand that Polk answer his questions, and, as he called the president "a bewildered, confounded, and miserably perplexed man," his opposition to the war became in itself controversial, with Illinois newspapers publishing a transcript of the January speech under the headline "Out Damned Spot."[8] Democratic papers called the speech unpatriotic; Lincoln, however, found a sympathetic ear with Greeley, who wrote in the *Tribune* that the Ashmun Amendment officially declared a manifest truth—that the president's war, as Lincoln had alleged, was unnecessary and unconstitutional.[9]

While in Washington, Lincoln read the *New York Tribune* regularly, and, growing to appreciate its attention to all things Whig, he in time was able to address the editor personally as "Friend Greeley." But at one point, he found the need to defend himself and attempt to correct the record. The fighting in Mexico had been over for months and the peace treaty signed when Lincoln, after reading in the *Tribune* a description of one of his speeches, wrote a letter to Greeley in June 1848, claiming the newspaper had made a mistake in telling readers that the boundary of Texas extended only to the Nueces River. "Now this is a mistake," Lincoln wrote, "which I dislike to see go uncorrected in a leading Whig paper." He insisted that the boundary of Texas extended "just so far as American settlements taking part in her revolution extended; and that as a matter of fact, those settlements did extend, at one or two points, beyond the Nueces, but not anywhere near to the Rio Grande at any point."[10] Greeley printed the letter in the *Tribune* without response, and Lincoln spent much of his remaining time in Congress and in following years clarifying his position. As late as 1858, the *Chicago Tribune*, his staunchest ally, found the need to editorialize that it was "a matter of profound indifference to the Republican party of Illinois" whether Lincoln had "voted for or against the Mexican war."[11]

Greeley, more quickly than had Lincoln, protested the Mexican-American War. Like Lincoln, he also took criticism, most vociferously from partisan editors—including his nemesis, James Gordon Bennett of the *New York Herald*, who praised Polk, writing, "The universal Yankee nation can regenerate and disenthrall the people of Mexico in a few years; and we believe it is a part of our destiny to civilize that beautiful country."[12] But Greeley also received praise from Whigs, including Senator Thomas Corwin of Ohio, who recognized that the *Tribune* was attracting antislavery advocates who saw the war as waged on behalf of southern slaveholders.[13] Greeley had filled the *Tribune* with horrific stories of American regiments cut to pieces, with piles of arms and legs stacked up by their enemies and camps surrounded by yellow fever and disease. He published a letter from a camp near Buena Vista, Mexico, that described barefoot marches through mud and water over hazardous surfaces and urged young men to read it before enlisting; he also flaunted a poem that depicted Mexicans as fiercely battling for their freedom against "the tyrant throng rushing from the land of slaves."[14]

At the same time, Greeley intensified his antislavery editorials, as he at first had opposed the institution as morally deficient and economically regressive and subsequently supported movements to prevent its extension. In addition to his opposition to the Mexican-American War, Greeley had approved of the Wilmot Proviso (1846)—a resolution popular among Whigs, including Lincoln— which, though never ratified, called for a ban on slavery in the territories taken from Mexico during the Mexican-American War. At about the same time, Greeley began juxtaposing slavery in the South with northern industrial labor, writing: "If I am less troubled concerning the slavery present in Charleston or New Orleans, it is because I see so much slavery in New York, which appears to claim my first efforts."[15] For Greeley, it was not necessary to cast slavery in terms of race; rather, the institution was a social condition in which an individual existed "mainly as a convenience for other human beings."[16]

Mr. Greeley Goes to Washington

With the end of the Mexican-American War and the addition of massive amounts of western land, the balance of representation in Washington shifted, challenging Thurlow Weed's position as the de facto head of the Whig Party. Although Weed might have promoted his friend William H. Seward as either a vice presidential or even a presidential candidate in 1848, he instead made the shrewd decision to support the nomination of war hero General Zachary Taylor. Dubbed "Old Rough and Ready" for his unassuming but effective demeanor and proven leadership in battle, Taylor had few (if any) previously known political affiliations. Lincoln had already, as early as August 1847, made known his support for Taylor (who was popularly received as a moderate) by giving speeches in support of the general and writing to newspapers, including the *Illinois Journal*, on his behalf. Weed, meanwhile, made additional concessions in acquiescing to the calls of Whigs to nominate Millard Fillmore, a conservative Whig from Buffalo, New York, for the role of vice president. In doing so, however, Weed took the opportunity to promote Seward for the Senate, which Seward first won in 1849 and again in 1855. Seward used the congressional pulpit to denounce slavery in speeches throughout the Northeast and Midwest, building upon aspirations for the presidency, which he would fervently seek (with Weed's help) in 1860.

Greeley supported Seward in his bid for the Senate, but he had no interest in using the *Tribune* to help elect Taylor, as he had already published volumes of antiwar material during the Mexican-American War, and promoting a general from that conflict would have contradicted his earlier views. Taylor supporters, aware of Greeley's role in shaping the opinions of readers, appealed to Greeley's sense of party loyalty and, knowing his deeply held desire for office, persuaded him to give a speech in September 1848 on Taylor's behalf at Vauxhall Garden, a fashionable entertainment area in Manhattan. In exchange, they made available to him a seat in Congress previously occupied by Democrat David S. Jackson.[17] Greeley, in turn, converted his ambivalence over Taylor into spoken support for him, informing the audience that he had promised he would support the Taylor nomination if it were the only way to defeat the Democrats.

Greeley's speech earned him the vacated House seat, a term that lasted only three months. But from December 1, 1848, to March 4, 1849, he took the appointment seriously and as one that would, he hoped, build upon his aspirations for other elected offices. While Lincoln had made news with his outspoken opposition to the war with Mexico, Greeley caused a stir in his attempts to style himself as a reform-minded activist. Before he had completed his first month in Congress, he embarked on a crusade (albeit a short one) against wasteful governmental spending. In December 1848, Greeley published shocking allegations in the *Tribune* that claimed his fellow legislators had bilked American taxpayers by charging unnecessary expenses to their accounts, with columns featuring lists of exorbitant expenses accrued by individual House members. Lincoln was on the list of violators because, Greeley claimed, the Illinois representative had submitted receipts for travel expenses totaling $676 more than he should have received, even though Greeley had based the claim on a travel route used by few living in the West.[18]

A more substantial effort to change public policy, which Greeley had advanced in previous *Tribune* columns calling for homestead settlements in the West, came with his promotion of a bill that discouraged speculation on public lands. Greeley championed efforts—although not immediately successful—to allow any citizen to own 160 acres of the new territories in the West, demonstrated in the land reform bill he introduced to the Committee on Public Lands.[19] Congress did not address the bill until February 27, 1849, with a fellow House member wanting to know why a New Yorker should busy himself with the disposition of the public domain. Greeley replied that he represented "more landless men than any other member."[20] Lincoln would not have the opportunity to vote "yea" or "nay" on Greeley's proposals, as only twenty members initially favored the bill and it was simply tabled; however, in 1862, Congress revisited the issue and passed the subsequently famous Homestead Act, which Lincoln, then president, ultimately signed into law.[21]

Clearly, Lincoln had issues of western lands in mind while he served in Congress, too, but not in the same sense that Greeley did. The Illinoisan had indicated to several friends that he had wanted to seek the position of commissioner of the General Land Office in Illinois, which paid a comfortable sum of three thousand dollars annually. The federally appointed post, one made by the president, ranked just below cabinet officers and carried prestige and some power; however, Lincoln changed his mind about pursuing it. Explaining his decision to David Davis, he said, "Taking the office would be a final surrender of the law, and that every man in the state, who wants it himself, would be snarling at me about it, I shrink from it."[22]

Preferring to bide his time in service to the Whigs by assisting others in their campaigns, Lincoln decided he would not return to the Illinois legislature or seek a higher elected (or appointed) office. He told William Herndon that he would seek a second term in Congress only if no other Whig sought the position (in the 1840s and 1850s, the average length of service for a U.S. Representative was three years, and there was no disgrace in serving one term). But whatever chance Lincoln might have had at reelection was summarily dismissed when his former law partner Stephen Trigg Logan decided to seek the Whig nomination.[23]

The Means to the End to Slavery

Lincoln and Greeley, meanwhile, in addition to their like-minded interest in federal land policy, worked together more closely on the legal status of slavery in what would become increasingly interrelated areas—in the United States and in the West. The two men were in very regular, if not constant, attendance upon the sessions of the House, and for the most part, their votes reflected common Whig philosophy, with their differences hardly reflecting opposition to each other but rather how to achieve shared goals.

On one level, different philosophical perspectives might explain the reasons for their votes. In December 1848, for example, a motion to permit the introduction of a bill that would ban slavery in Washington, D.C., had been defeated in an 82–70 vote, with Greeley voting "yea" and Lincoln "nay." Only days later, the House approved a different bill that would have allowed for the people who lived in the nation's capital to express their wishes on the continuation of slavery. This time, Lincoln cast a "yea" and Greeley a "nay."[24]

While Lincoln believed that the people of Washington should decide the issue and Greeley believed that the federal government should lead, upon further examination, their rationales might also demonstrate deeper, more complicated political maneuverings. When, on December 21, 1848, Lincoln first joined three other northern Whigs in opposing the resolution of Daniel Gott, a New York representative who had called for the ban on slavery in Washington, D.C., his reasons for doing so are not entirely clear. Lincoln was unsuccessful in attempting to table the resolution, and his actions drew criticism from Ohio's Joshua R. Giddings, who said that Lincoln had in effect voted to support the slave trade. But Lincoln's opposition had apparently stemmed from his reading of its preamble, which he thought was too abrasive—language that had come from none other than the editor of the *New York Tribune*. Greeley, who had persuaded Gott to adopt the language, stated that the slave trade in the District was "contrary to natural justice" and "notoriously a reproach to our country throughout Christendom and a serious hindrance to the progress of republican liberty among the nations of the earth." Yet, while Lincoln indeed voted against the resolution, historian Michael Burlingame notes it is possible that he did so because he was preparing an even stronger resolution of his own.[25]

Before Greeley had even arrived in Washington, Lincoln had already resolved to act upon his convictions about slavery. Lincoln had supported the Wilmot Proviso, as had Greeley, and Lincoln voted for it, he later said, "at least forty times during the short time I was there."[26] However, in addition to his support for the proviso, Lincoln had also decided to seek a bold measure in the nation's capital, calling for a ban on slavery. The introduction of the bill in the House in January 1849 caused a stir, but it clearly was not something Lincoln proposed out of simple political expediency. He had ruminated over the suggestion for at least ten years, having suggested as a member of the Illinois General Assembly in 1837 that he believed Congress had the legal authority to abolish slavery in the capital but that the power ought not be exercised unless at the request of the people who lived there. Although little came of Lincoln's bill—he backed away from it upon realizing it lacked support—it did illustrate his willingness to take a strong position on an unpopular issue.

After vigorous objections to revisions in the original Gott resolution, including threats of disunion from southern representatives, the House ended discussion on the measure by voting to drop it from further discussion. Reflecting on Lincoln's final vote against the measure, a "no," Greeley later described him quite simply as "one of the very mildest type of Wilmot Proviso Whigs from the free States." However, Greeley did object to Lincoln's provision that would have required voters in the District to vote on emancipation and wrote, "It seemed to me much like submitting to a vote of the inmates of a penitentiary a proposition to double the length of their respective terms of imprisonment."[27]

Lincoln had little to say about his experiences with Greeley in the House, but the man who as president would later sign the Greeley-inspired Homestead Act at first had not left a dramatic impression on Greeley, either. Greeley would later write autobiographically of Lincoln simply as "a genial, cheerful, rather comely man, noticeably tall, and the only Whig from Illinois, not remarkable otherwise."[28] Regardless, the two eventually formed a relationship that differed occasionally on the means to reach their respective goals but at the same time worked toward the twin ends of Union and freedom.

As Lincoln's term neared its end, the allegations made by the *Tribune* about his travel expenditures concerned him far less than the fallout from the Spot Resolutions. His opponents had dubbed him "Spotty Lincoln," and as veterans from the war returned to Lincoln's home district in large numbers, they chose the Democratic candidate over him. Lincoln's House speeches had detractors, but, contrary to what William Herndon had reported in Illinois, most of the criticism came not from Whigs but from Democratic newspapers. Among the few Whigs who might have held Lincoln responsible for the loss of his seat to the Democrats, Caleb Birchall, a Springfield bookseller, said only that Lincoln had "rendered himself very unpopular." While Lincoln's positions would not have necessarily made a bid for reelection an easy one, he had already pledged to step down, and while many of his initial supporters admired his principled stand and favored his renomination, they instead named him to serve as an assistant presidential elector.[29]

With Greater Earnestness Than Ever Before

Beginning in 1848, the physical journeys of Lincoln and Greeley recurrently crossed, with both of them having attended as unofficial observers the June 1848 Whig convention in Philadelphia that nominated Taylor. The two, in biographer Harlan Hoyt Horner's estimation, represented opposite spectrums of the party—while Lincoln sought political realism, Greeley provided idealism.[30] Neither Lincoln nor Greeley, both of whom remained at the time lifelong advocates of Henry Clay, could support the elder statesman for what would have been a fourth presidential bid. Lincoln, having already recognized that the Kentuckian's chances for the presidency had escaped him in the previous election, devoted his efforts to helping Taylor secure the nomination instead. Greeley, however, upon discovering the objectives of the Taylor campaign—or the lack thereof (in an effort to achieve some measure of national unity, leaders had developed a noncommittal platform that avoided the issue of slavery)—virtually disassociated himself from the Whig Party. Greeley dubbed the Taylor platform "the slaughterhouse of Whig principles" because it ignored the Wilmot Proviso, and when the convention abandoned support for it also, he wrote, "I felt my zeal, my enthusiasm for the Whig cause was laid out there also."[31]

The division within the Whig ranks was less politically complicated than the problems facing Democrats. In nominating Senator Lewis Cass of Michigan—a leading proponent of the doctrine of Squatter (or Popular) Sovereignty, which would have allowed settlers in new territories to determine the status of slavery—the party nearly imploded over its insistence on meeting the expansionist issues still tied to the Mexican-American War. President Polk, at the same time, failed to popularize his successes, including the reestablishment of the Independent Treasury System, the reduction of tariffs, the acquisition of parts of the Oregon Country from the British, and the acquisition of California and New Mexico from Mexico.[32]

During Cass's campaign, the Democrats had tried to use land, a tangible asset—specifically the areas of the West that they had wrested from Mexico and Native Americans—to recruit followers. The Whigs had meanwhile discovered that compromise was no formula for long-term success. In the East, especially, they sought to attract new voters to an otherwise precarious platform—one that sought to attract everyone by offending no one—with added appeals to the interests of the growing Irish and German voting bloc.[33]

Greeley's primary audience remained the workers of Manhattan's Sixth Ward, home of the *Tribune* office, but he also integrated news of direct concern to the area's new inhabitants. On one occasion, he praised participants in a Whig rally, describing them as "not properly Native nor Adopted Citizens, Yankees, Germans, Irish nor Welsh, but all Americans and nothing else."[34] He tailored the *Tribune*'s antislavery message to audiences that were receptive not only to racial and ethnic issues but to economic ones as well. "Free Americans do not want to go to the far West, there to work by the side of the miserable slave, with the overseer's lash continually in his eye," Greeley wrote. "Irishmen and Germans do not leave the horrors of feudal aristocracy to help to spread a viler and meaner yoke over this free Continent."[35]

On Election Day, the Democrats were unable to sell their successes in the West to an electorate soured by the Mexican-American War, losing at least in part because Martin Van Buren, as a Free Soil candidate—a third party devoted to advancing both free labor and the prevention of slavery's extension—garnered more than 10 percent of the vote. In a victory few anticipated, Taylor won the required electoral votes of eight slave states and seven free states, with 47.3 percent of the popular vote.

Henry Clay, after failing to win the 1848 presidential nomination, retired from politics (or so he intended) and returned to his Ashland estate in Lexington, Kentucky. But during the debates over the admission of new states in the West, he was asked to serve his country for a final time in the Senate. With Whigs generally believing that Congress ought to lead the president rather than the other way around, Clay returned to Washington, both because he felt that the country needed him and because he thought Taylor lacked the experience and political skills needed in a president. Congress convened in December 1849, and in January 1850, Clay gave a speech that called for compromise on the issues dividing the Union. Even though Congress did not adopt his specific proposals for achieving a compromise, he could claim credit for drafting legislation, later dubbed the Compromise of 1850, which he essentially did write.

The legislative package featured the notion, advanced by Senator Stephen A. Douglas of Illinois, that territorial governments should exercise popular sovereignty—the same idea that the Democrats had promoted in their unsuccessful 1848 campaign for Lewis Cass. The complex legislative package provided for the admission of California as a free state, the organization of the New Mexico and Utah territories without mention of slavery, the abolition of the slave trade in the District of Columbia, and a powerful federal fugitive slave law designed to restore runaway slaves back to their masters. Always a great admirer of Clay—and of his role in at least inspiring the legislation—Lincoln personally approved of the measures, but most northern Whigs, including Seward, Weed, and Greeley, opposed them because they did not allow for a ban on the extension of slavery. While antislavery advocates were outraged especially by the provision that allowed masters to repossess slaves who had escaped to free states, President Taylor attempted to sidestep the entire controversy by pushing for the immediate admission of California and New Mexico as free states.

The president had said privately to Seward and Weed that he would "strongly rebuke disunionists" over the issue, but before he—or anyone—had the chance to see whether the Compromise of 1850 would accomplish its goals, tragedy again visited the Whigs.[36] Taylor, a lifelong admirer of George Washington, attended the July 4, 1850, event that set the cornerstone of the Washington Monument. After sitting for hours in the hot sun, Taylor drank large quantities of ice water, ate cherries with iced milk, and later that night suffered what doctors described as a cholera attack. Five days later, he died, making him the second—and final—Whig president to die in office. The Whig Party, although it had won the presidency in two of the three previous elections and enjoyed congressional majorities throughout the 1840s, never recovered. Vice President Millard Fillmore assumed the presidency, and although a Whig, he saw the antislavery movement as an obstacle to national harmony. In one devastating motion, as Weed described it, Fillmore signed the 1850 Fugitive Slave Law and rendered the Whig Party "in twain forever."[37]

With Taylor's death marking the waning influence of the Whigs, Greeley in the interim reconsidered his views about the late president, reflecting that Taylor had demonstrated admirable resolve when little was expected. "General Taylor died too soon for his country's good," Greeley wrote, "but not till he had proved himself a wise and good ruler, if not even a great one."[38] Lincoln, meanwhile, had returned to Illinois with little to say about his congressional experience—to this day, few documents about his thoughts on politics exist from this period—but he did deliver a memorable eulogy for Taylor in Chicago, marked by haunting, if not foreshadowing, words. "I will not pretend to believe that all the wisdom, or all the patriotism of the country, died with Gen. Taylor," he said. "But we know that wisdom and patriotism, in a public office, under institutions like ours, are wholly inefficient and worthless, unless they are sustained by the confidence and devotion of the people. And I confess my apprehensions, that in the death of the late President, we have lost a degree of that confidence and devotion, which will not soon again pertain to any successor."[39]

Taylor's death was the next in a series of Whig misfortunes that would climax two years later with the loss of nominee Winfield Scott as the party's final presidential candidate. In June 1852, Henry Clay—whom Lincoln and Greeley in 1844 had worked tirelessly in vain to elect president—died at the age of seventy-five. Just a few months later, Daniel Webster, another Whig giant who had served his country as a statesman and as a leader in the Senate, also died. By the time of the November election, voters had wearied of the Whig formula of nominating war heroes, and Scott, another Mexican-American War general, was old and not that popular after all.

On the day after Clay's death, Greeley had devoted the entire editorial page of the *Tribune* to eulogies with columns encased in heavy black borders. Clay had sought "national greatness and glory,"

Greeley wrote, "through the facilitation and cheapening of international intercourse, the creation of new branches of industry, the improvement of national resources, rather than through the devastation of foreign territories and the dismemberment of foreign countries."[40] He concurrently edited and issued an entire biographical volume of Clay's speeches and works (compiled by author and poet Epes Sargent) with additional reflections, among his most astute not only on Clay's career but also on the condition of national affairs. "We Americans of 1852—nearly all of us who read or think, with many who do neither—are the heated partisans or embittered opponents of Mr. Clay—with him or against him, idolizing or detesting him, we have struggled through all the past decades of our manhood," Greeley wrote. "He has been our demigod or demon through the last quarter of a century . . . but we, who knew and loved him well, may more truly and vividly, even though awkwardly and feebly, depict how looked and felt, how spoke and acted, how lived and loved, the man Henry Clay."[41]

Lincoln also delivered a powerful eulogy to Clay, emphasizing in spoken words the devotion to liberty of the Kentuckian who had inspired Lincoln at an early age. In another melancholic reflection, reminiscent of his Taylor eulogy, Lincoln concluded that the nation's fate teetered on the decisions of men such as Clay, who, it must have seemed, were leaving their followers in a most untimely fashion. Raising Clay to near superhuman status, Lincoln reflected: "Henry Clay belonged to his country—to the world; mere party cannot claim men like him. . . . Let us strive to deserve, as far as mortals may, the continued care of Divine Providence, trusting that in future national emergencies, He will not fail to provide us the instruments of safety and security."[42]

Lincoln by necessity also addressed a problematic aspect of Clay's life. "He ever was on principle and in feeling opposed to slavery," Lincoln said. "And yet Mr. Clay was the owner of slaves." Echoing what Greeley had written about the conflicting perspectives on not only Clay's career but also the increasingly volatile issue of slavery, Lincoln sought to appreciate the predicament of southerners. "Those who would shiver into fragments the Union of these States, tear to tatters its now venerated Constitution, and even burn the last copy of the Bible, rather than slavery should continue a single hour, together with all their more halting sympathizers, have received, and are receiving, their just execration," Lincoln said. "[A]nd the name and opinions and influence of Mr. Clay are fully and, as I trust, effectually and enduringly arrayed against them."[43]

In the wake of Whig calamities, Lincoln wrote that he had studied law "with greater earnestness than ever before."[44] However, when Congress passed the Kansas-Nebraska Act in 1854—in yet another attempt to address issues at the heart of the Compromise of 1850—he made a decisive return to politics. The legislation nullified the Missouri Compromise (a legal agreement that had mediated the slavery issue for more than thirty years) and marked an increase in the urgency of events and political developments throughout the rest of the decade. The formation of the Republican Party, the outbreak of violence in both Kansas and in the Senate, and John Brown's raid on Harpers Ferry shaped not only Lincoln's career but Greeley's as well, along with the very annals of history.

Abraham Lincoln, Congressman-Elect from Illinois, Library of Congress. Created in Springfield, Illinois, in either 1846 or 1847, this daguerreotype is the earliest known photograph of Abraham Lincoln, taken at age thirty-seven, when he was a frontier lawyer in Springfield and congressman-elect from Illinois. The photo is attributed to Nicholas H. Shepherd of Springfield, according to the recollections of Gibson W. Harris, a law student in Lincoln's office from 1845 to 1847. Robert Lincoln, son of the president, thought it was made in either St. Louis or Washington during his father's term in Congress.

Horace Greeley, Library of Congress. A photographer affiliated with Mathew Brady's studios took this daguerreotype of Horace Greeley sometime between 1844 and 1860, according to the Library of Congress's archives. Because later photos of Greeley show him with a neck beard, this image of him sitting with a newspaper folded on his lap was most likely taken in the 1840s, shortly after he launched the *New York Tribune*.

LOG CABIN BUILT BY PRESIDENT LINCOLN IN KENTUCKY.—SKETCHED BY L. HURZ.

Log Cabin Built by President Lincoln in Kentucky, from *Frank Leslie's Illustrated Newspaper*, vol. 20, July 8, 1865, p. 256, Library of Congress. The popular newspaper, among the few of the era to contain illustrations, published this rendition of the slain president's boyhood home within months of his death. Although the Lincoln family left Kentucky when Abraham was a boy, the imagery of the frontier had become so indelibly connected to his legacy that the artist here presumed young Abraham had actually built the log cabin himself.

Log Cabin, May 2, 1840, courtesy of the Rare Book, Manuscript, and Special Collections Library at Duke University. The front page from this issue of Horace Greeley's *Log Cabin* includes a portrait of William Henry Harrison and columns that promote his presidential campaign. It represents the typical layout of content in Greeley's famous publication, which included illustrations of Harrison's exploits in battle, songs from his campaign, and lively editorials that promoted "Old Tippecanoe" for president.

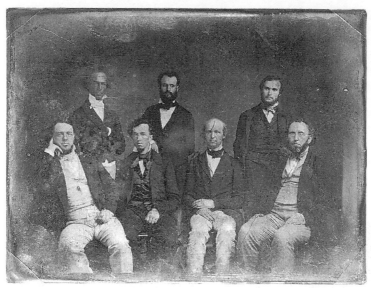

"Editorial Staff of the *New York Tribune*," Library of Congress. Seated (*left to right*) are George M. Snow, financial editor; Bayard Taylor, renowned literary critic; Horace Greeley; and George Ripley, literary editor. Standing (*left to right*) are William Henry Fry, music editor; Charles A. Dana, who became Greeley's managing editor; and Henry J. Raymond, former assistant to Greeley. Taken sometime between 1844 and 1860, according to Library of Congress archivists, the photo is remarkable inasmuch as it shows Raymond, who left the *Tribune* in 1841 and later became Greeley's rival as editor of the *New York Times*, together with Greeley.

MARK ANTONY RAYMOND   CASCA BLAIR.
CÆSAR SEWARD.   BRUTUS GREELEY.

"ET TU, GREELEY?"

Et Tu, Greeley?, *Vanity Fair*, June 2, 1860, courtesy of Special
Collections/Musselman Library, Gettysburg College,
Gettysburg, Pennsylvania. In May 1860, delegates at the
Republican National Convention abandoned front-runner
William H. Seward and chose Abraham Lincoln as their
presidential nominee. In this cartoon, *Vanity Fair* compares
the turn of events to Julius Caesar's assassination in the Roman
Senate (likely relying on Shakespeare's interpretation). Seward, as
Caesar, lies dying on the floor, having been stabbed by *New York
Tribune* editor Horace Greeley (Brutus). The artist depicts *New
York Times* editor Henry Raymond as Mark Antony and Francis
Blair Sr., editor of the *Congressional Record*, as Casca. Lincoln
is portrayed as a small black man. ("Black Republican" was a
derogatory term used to associate the party with abolitionism.)

THE SLAUGHTER OF SEWARD.

The Slaughter of Seward, from the *Campaign Plain Dealer*, July 7, 1860, the Lincoln Financial Foundation Collection, courtesy of the Indiana State Museum. Chicago was known for its stockyards and slaughterhouses, and this cartoon from a Cleveland newspaper that supported Stephen A. Douglas used the analogy of a cattle slaughterhouse for the Republican National Convention in Chicago. Presidential nominee Abraham Lincoln prepares to knock out the party's brains, represented by William H. Seward, the front-runner whom Lincoln defeated. The editors of three leading New York newspapers are (*left to right*) James Watson Webb of the *New York Courier and Enquirer*, Thurlow Weed of the *Albany Evening Journal*, and Horace Greeley of the *New York Tribune*. Weed provided significant support for Seward, as evidenced by his shock in the cartoon, while Webb covers his eyes, too frightened to watch. "Just what you deserve," says the satisfied Greeley, who had helped to ensure both Seward's defeat and Lincoln's victory.

The Last Rail Split by "Honest Old Abe."

The Last Rail Split by "Honest Old Abe," from
Wide-Awake Pictorial, November 1, 1860, p. 6,
Library of Congress. To appeal to average voters,
Republicans emphasized the poor, hardworking
origin of Abraham Lincoln, depicting him as
a rail splitter. This cartoon plays on that image
by showing that his 1860 nomination split the
Democratic Party.

Abraham Lincoln to Horace Greeley, August 22, 1862, courtesy of Caroline Welling Van Deusen. President Lincoln's reply to Greeley's *Tribune* editorial "The Prayer of Twenty Millions" was submitted for publication to James Clarke Welling, editor of the *National Intelligencer*. Van Deusen, Welling's great-granddaughter, made this letter available for reproduction here. Greeley had called on the president to emancipate the slaves, and Lincoln's letter signaled to readers that he believed his first task was to preserve the Union. The letter made no mention, however, that he had already decided privately to issue the Emancipation Proclamation. While Greeley earned credit for raising the issue of abolition to one that the public would recognize as an important aspect of the war, and what I forbear, I forbear because I do *not* believe it would help to save the Union. I shall do *less* whenever I shall believe what I am doing hurts the cause, and I shall do *more* whenever I shall believe doing more will help the cause. I shall try to correct errors when shown to be errors; and I shall adopt new views so fast as they shall appear to be true views.

I have here stated my purpose according to my view of *official* duty; and I intend no modification of my oft-expressed *personal* wish that all men everywhere could be free.

Yours.
A. Lincoln

Lincoln demonstrated his ability to manage important wartime information as well as editors. Remarkably, Welling determined it necessary to delete the sentence on page 2 that reads, "Broken eggs can never be mended, and the longer the breaking proceeds the more will be broken." See Lincoln to Greeley, August 22, 1862, in Basler, *Collected Works*, 5:388–89.

Dedication Ceremonies at the Soldiers' National Cemetery, Gettysburg, Pennsylvania, Library of Congress. Historians have recently suggested that this previously obscure image by Alexander Gardner is one of only two known photos of President Lincoln at the 1863 commemoration. In 2007, members of the Center for Civil War Photography determined that Lincoln might be visible in the crowd—just to the right of the arch gateway—when viewed through magnification. The other photo of Lincoln at Gettysburg, part of the Mathew Brady Collection in the National Archives and Records Administration, was identified in 1952 as a hurried and unfocused shot taken by David Bachrach.

CHAPTER THREE

FREE SOIL, FREE LABOR,
FREE SPEECH, FREE MEN

By accident, the saying "Go West, young man, go West" would come to be attributed to Horace Greeley, but in the spring of 1859, Greeley took the advice and set off to explore the area. The previous year, he had upset readers in Illinois—until that time considered part of the West—by supporting Stephen A. Douglas, whom, although a Democrat, Republicans in the East saw as someone who could help their chances in the 1860 election. As Greeley traveled west, he took extensive, reporter-like notes along the way and published them under the title *An Overland Journey from New York to San Francisco*. The documentary described such areas as his initial stop in Kansas and detailed his travels over the American Plains to the Rocky Mountains, throughout Colorado, into the Mormon areas of Utah, including Salt Lake, and then to California.

Greeley had traveled west in part to survey the projected central route for a transcontinental railroad, but it also provided him the opportunity to see firsthand areas he had previously only written about in editorials. He discovered that the region, which he had personally romanticized as an area in which an individual could live free (and by Henry Clay's ideals of self-made reliance), had living conditions that were in some ways as treacherous as those of urban New York. The plains were, he wrote with surprise, an area of "sterility and thirst," yet he tirelessly reported in letters published in the *Tribune* the economic possibilities of the West for farmers, miners, ranchers, and merchants.[1] By the end of the year, he would also find his ideal candidate for the 1860 presidency—not in the East but in a western candidate like no other, Abraham Lincoln.

While traditional accounts of Lincoln's presidential bid detail his rise from life in a humble log cabin to his famous campaign as "The Rail Splitter," less mythic events based in intense and sometimes petty political rivalries, both with roots in early-nineteenth-century partisan formations, played an equal role in his ascent. The transitional period of the 1850s included interrelated events—the collapse of the Whig Party, the development of the Republican Party, and the establishment of the Third Party System of American politics—from which a rivalry between the Republican and Democratic Parties emerged. The configuration survived the Civil War, and although it still exists today, at the time the two groups confronted issues that were remarkably different—and much more volatile—than anything before or since.

Likewise, the careers that Lincoln and Greeley developed during the period, although both entirely based in the Republican Party, formed a mixture of policies and ideas much more combustible than their previous relationship would suggest. While Lincoln at one moment felt betrayed by Greeley's lack of support in his 1858 bid for the Senate, he was alternately surprised to receive Greeley's support in his 1860 bid for the Republican nomination. Greeley, meanwhile, while reaping acclaim for his success in promoting Lincoln throughout 1860, also felt betrayed when the president did not reciprocate with an appointment to his cabinet.

The most consistent source of support for Lincoln instead came from the *Chicago Tribune*, first published in 1847, which, because of its obvious geographical advantage, contributed directly to his success in the Republican convention in none other than the West's new burgeoning version of Gotham. At the same time, Lincoln could not have succeeded on a national level without a network that linked Illinois to the East. Much to the chagrin of New York's Republicans, who had expected a William H. Seward presidency in 1860, the final surge in votes necessary for Lincoln's nomination came from one of their own: Greeley. Although the link between Lincoln and Greeley in Chicago in 1860 subtly resembled the role of the two men at the

Chicago River and Harbor Convention in 1847, it marked another turning point in their increasingly consequential roles as national figures, as both men continued to live according to their understanding of what Henry Clay had described as self-made destinies.

Thunderstruck and Stunned

During his six years away from politics following a term in the U.S. House, Lincoln reimmersed himself in literature, reading on a level in which he had not indulged since the nights he spent by firelight as a boy. His biographer and law partner at the time, William Herndon, observed that Lincoln carried with him a well-worn copy of Shakespeare, which Lincoln read in leisure moments, and that he had grown fond of the literary style of Edgar Allan Poe.[2] Lincoln memorized the melancholic poem "Mortality" by William Knox and recited its verses so well that listeners thought he had written it himself. Even though Lincoln did not know the name of the original writer until later in his life, he once remarked, "I would give all I am worth, and go in debt, to be able to write so fine a piece as I think that is."[3]

While Lincoln was away in Washington, Herndon had maintained the law office in which he and Lincoln had established a partnership in 1844, and when Lincoln returned to Springfield in 1849, the two men resumed working together as partners. The legal climate in Illinois had changed throughout the 1840s, as the courts institutionalized daily proceedings and, as Herndon described it, depended less on "the pyrotechnics of courtroom and stump oratory." The change in the tone of the courtroom coincided with a change in Lincoln's attitude toward politics, as his disassociation from Congress had made him more practically oriented and concerned with daily business matters. The change was noticeable, as he sought a more disciplined approach—"a want of mental training and method," Herndon wrote. "He was not soured at his seeming political decline, but still he determined to eschew politics from that time forward and devote himself entirely to the law."[4]

Others—not merely Lincoln alone—shared the changes in political sensibilities as, in the early 1850s, conservatives, moderates, and progressives alike had begun to abandon the once vibrant, recurrently whimsical Whig Party. Zachary Taylor's death, combined with Millard Fillmore's reversal of many Whig initiatives, had alienated previous supporters. By the outset of the 1852 presidential campaign, only nine of the seventy-five Whig newspapers in New York supported Fillmore, with Greeley having already determined that the Whigs should support another Mexican-American War hero, General Winfield Scott, for the 1852 nomination.[5] In addition to signing the Compromise of 1850, which had upset many Whigs who viewed the action as a betrayal of Taylor (who had opposed it), Fillmore had demonstrated his apparent sympathy for the growing nativist movement by opposing accommodations for millions of new immigrants, a potentially new but otherwise forsaken constituency.

Slavery more than any other issue had split the Whigs, North and South, and the deaths of two presidents in less than ten years had shaken voter confidence. During the June 1852 Whig national convention in Baltimore, debate degenerated over minor questions, and after fifty-two failed nomination attempts, delegates finally selected Winfield Scott, who had—too much like Taylor, it would turn out—made fame for himself during the Mexican-American War. His moniker, "Old Fuss and Feathers," said more about the way he carried himself in public than it did about his political views, but from even the fairest accounts, he had grown old and so large that he could no longer even ride a horse.

Greeley, for his part, attempted to rouse an apathetic electorate with enthusiastic accounts of Scott's campaign speeches. But critics of the *Tribune*—even fellow Whigs—had grown increasingly dubious of the newspaper's content, as Greeley had continued to promote protectionism, and specifically a tariff on imported goods, as a primary Whig tenet and as a way to build a strong American labor force, even though most in the party had ceased to emphasize it years ago. In fact, the Whigs struggled to consistently address any issue during the campaign, whether immigration or western expansion, slavery or the role of free labor, leaving the *Boston Pilot*, a staunchly Catholic and by definition antinativist newspaper, to dismiss Greeley's efforts to campaign on Scott's behalf as a baseless appeal to "Protection or No Protection."[6]

Sensing the direction of the 1852 election, Greeley published a tract titled *Why I Am a Whig*, articulating his steadfast opposition to Democrats. It described little in the Whig platform but noted that, from Jackson and Van Buren to Tyler and Polk, the opponents of free labor had rewarded slavelike subservience to "Caesar" with a system of spoils that included the extension of slavery to new territories. He suggested that the Democrats enjoyed an undeserved advantage simply because they had a name that was more popularly recognized—one that "the most ignorant comprehends, in which the most depressed finds promise of hope and sympathy, and which the humble and lowly immigrant, just landed from his Atlantic voyage, recognizes as the watchword of liberty."[7]

The Democrats also had difficulty at their convention in choosing a candidate who represented their interests, but after forty-nine ballot attempts, they selected Franklin Pierce—like Scott, an inexperienced politician, but unlike Scott, young and charismatic. Pierce, a New Hampshire senator, had at least held office. Voters chose personality over politics, and amid confusing allegations of Scott's connections to nativists, his denials of those allegations, and his failure to associate himself with any position in particular—except for being antislavery—the Whigs carried only four of thirty-one states (Massachusetts, Vermont, Kentucky, and Tennessee). Pierce won the rest and scored an electoral landslide. In a precursor to the next election, the Free Soil Party, with John P. Hale as its presidential candidate, had emerged on a platform more clearly opposing the extension of slavery than that of the Whigs to gain 5 percent of the popular vote, including the support of northern Democrats who had defected from the party over increasingly regional interests.

In response, former Whigs and antislavery Democrats looked to the platform of the Free Soil Party, which, after a notable entrance in the elections of 1848 and 1852, had reemerged as the debates over Popular Sovereignty reached the question of whether Kansas, having organized petitions for statehood, would develop a constitution that allowed or banned slavery. They also looked for a party that would both take the place of the Whigs and form a stronger opposition to what they saw as the Democratic stranglehold on Congress. The party at first gradually emerged in early 1854, as the first meeting of what would eventually become the Republican Party took place in Ripon, Wisconsin, in response to the Kansas-Nebraska legislation, which Congress passed on May 30, 1854. Although historians have recognized varying accounts that describe the origin of the name "Republican," Greeley deserves credit at least for popularizing it, if not for being the very first to use it. "We should not much care whether those thus united were designated 'Whig,' 'Free Democratic,' or something else," he wrote in a June 1854 editorial, "though we think some simple name like 'Republican' would more fitly designate those who had united to restore our union to its true mission of champion and promulgator of Liberty rather than propagandist of Slavery."[8]

Popular outrage—epitomized by a mass rally on June 6, 1854, of 10,000 people who met on the outskirts of Jackson, Michigan—took the form of demonstrations and scathing newspaper editorials following the decision of Congress to allow settlers to determine by popular vote the legality or illegality of slavery in areas where it had previously been banned. More than any other event since leaving Congress, Lincoln later wrote, it was this decision— the Kansas Nebraska Act— that motivated him (more accurately, outraged him) into reentering the political arena. Upon hearing news of the legislation, he not only joined the growing movement of Republicans in opposing the extension of slavery but encouraged others to do so as well.

Lincoln gave two extraordinary speeches at Springfield and Peoria two weeks apart in 1854, marking his reentry into the politics of Illinois and catapulting him into the debates over slavery that dominated state and national politics for the rest of the decade. Lincoln delivered the substance of these arguments several times—certainly in Springfield on October 4, 1854, for which there are only press reports. A longer version came twelve days later in Peoria, a speech with content that—more than any other, according to historian Lewis Lehrman—raised his stature as a potential presidential candidate.[9] With characteristic calmness and restraint, Lincoln spoke in the October 16 speech with his strongest antislavery statements up to that point in time. He directly addressed the legislation that his opponent Stephen A. Douglas had helped to pass, not simply objecting to its inevitable consequences but issuing a call to action unlike anything he had ever done as a Whig. "We were thunderstruck and stunned, and we reeled and fell in utter confusion," Lincoln said. "But we rose, each fighting, grasping whatever he could first reach—a scythe, a pitchfork, a chopping ax, or a butcher's cleaver."[10]

The three-hour speech, according to Lincoln's contemporaries, marked a new understanding on his part of the nature of politics and of slavery. He continued to maintain a detached rationalism in understanding the limits of reform the Constitution allowed, but he also recognized that the concept of compromise had died with the Whigs. Although Lincoln allowed room for concession on matters of policy, at least in order to maintain some level of national unity, he began to pursue in earnest the goal of establishing a Union that would not permit the extension of slavery but would instead cause the institution to eventually wither and die.

Lincoln's reentry into politics did not consist of speeches alone. In late 1854, he made a decision to run for the U.S. Senate as a Whig but came to recognize the need for establishing the Republican Party instead. His own statements about the wedge in the Whig Party that the Kansas-Nebraska Act had caused reflected a larger national condition. "I think I am a Whig, but others say there are no Whigs, and I am an abolitionist, even though I do no more than oppose the expansion of slavery," he wrote.[11] Despite leading as a Senate candidate in the first six rounds of voting in the state legislature, Lincoln instructed his backers to switch their support to Lyman Trumbull, which would prevent Joel Aldrich Matteson, a candidate who supported Douglas's legislation, from winning.[12] While the tactics were successful and Trumbull won, Lincoln, who in the process had turned down a seat in the Illinois legislature to help Trumbull, secured favor with Republicans as their pick for the next Senate opportunity.

For the remainder of the 1850s, Lincoln devoted his interests to advancing the Republican Party, suggesting it was time to end the rhetorical debates about the status of slavery in the West and reach a conclusion on whether it would be allowed to exist there. Lincoln wanted a ban on the spread of slavery, and an August 1855 letter he wrote to his friend Joshua Speed, who had owned slaves and at the time had no sympathy for Lincoln's position on the issue, described his desire to act upon the issue instead of brooding over it. "It is hardly fair for you to assume, that I have no interest in a thing which has, and continually exercises, the power of making me miserable," Lincoln wrote, referring of course to slavery. "You ought rather to appreciate how much the great body of the Northern people do crucify their feelings, in order to maintain their loyalty to the constitution and the Union."[13]

Republican Firsts

The Republicans held their first state party convention in Michigan in July 1854 and by 1856 were prepared to nominate their first candidate for the presidency. In February, Greeley attended the party's national organizational meeting in Pittsburgh, and in June, with Greeley's rival Henry Raymond of the *Times* playing a prominent role in the proceedings, the Republicans nominated John C. Frémont as their first candidate for president. The platform they drafted included ideas that had been associated with free labor, free soil, and, to a lesser extent, protectionism. The *Philadelphia Public Ledger* reported that a delegate from Illinois had nominated a still relatively unknown national figure, Abraham Lincoln, for vice president, saying only that he was "a good fellow, a firm friend of freedom and an old line Whig."[14] On an informal ballot, Lincoln received 110 votes for the role, but in the formal vote, William Dayton, a former New Jersey senator, secured the spot.

Senator Seward of New York had by then delivered one of his most famous speeches on the need for the citizenry to recognize a "Higher Law" that transcended the Constitution and forbade slavery. In 1856—and perhaps even before then—Seward had clearly wanted to run for the presidency, but recognizing that the party's chances at an actual victory were small, he, on the encouragement of his senior advisor, Thurlow Weed, opted out of the race. Weed, in cultivating Seward's presidential aspirations, naturally expected support from Greeley, who had worked on previous campaigns for Whig (and now Republican) candidates. Weed, however, was unaware of how deeply upset Greeley had grown over years of neglect at the hands of his partners, who Greeley believed had failed to support him in his own political aspirations. He had asked Weed to nominate him for New York governor in 1854, but Weed declined, recognizing that Greeley's affiliation with the temperance movement could cost the party much-needed votes. After seeing his rival Henry Raymond of the upstart *Times* advance in Whig circles, receiving the post of lieutenant governor, while he, a longtime supporter of Seward's, had remained relegated to the role of publicist, Greeley felt his time was due. Writing a bitter resignation letter (addressed to Seward) that dissolved his connection to the "firm" of Seward, Weed, and Greeley, the latter rationalized the move by suggesting in the letter that Seward and Weed had outgrown the need for his services.[15]

Frémont, as expected, did not win in 1856, suffering in part from unsubstantiated allegations that he was either Catholic or born out of wedlock, or both. Anti-immigrant sentiments had grown throughout the early 1850s, with waves of settlers having fled parts of Europe in the late 1840s for parts of the Northeast and Midwest to compete with laborers for jobs. Although the alleged evidence of Frémont's ties to Roman papacy were spurious at best—he had long attended a Protestant church and had baptized his children as Protestants— the perception of an outside threat on the United States resonated with the Democratic supporters of James Buchanan, a well-known Pennsylvania statesman with southern sympathies.

Despite the negative attacks and his relatively short political résumé, Frémont maintained a charismatic reputation as "The Pathfinder" for his extensive navigation of settlement routes in the West, and in the election, he surpassed the expectations of many Republicans by winning eleven out of thirty-one states and 114 electoral votes to Buchanan's 174. Lincoln's response, hardly one of despair, consoled Chicago Republicans, preparing them for a more favorable rematch. "Let us re-inaugurate the good old 'central ideas' of the Republic. We can do it," he said. "The human heart *is* with us—God is with us. We shall again be able not to declare, that 'all States as States, are equal,' or yet that 'all citizens are equal,' but to renew the broader better declaration, including these and much more, that 'all *men* are created equal.'"[16] Republicans evidently took the advice, adopting the slogan used in 1856, "Free Soil, Free Labor, Free Speech, Free Men, and Frémont," as the slogan for their efforts in the next election, although few expected Frémont to run again. However, having forged the path for Lincoln to follow, his campaign had made possible the ascendancy of other candidates with western interests clearly at the forefront of their agenda.

Buchanan entered office with hopes that his extensive diplomatic experience would bring a measure of stability to the tensions in the West. But for the next four years, national troubles only worsened as the new administration failed—in many ways, more dramatically than the previous one—to address the problems of Kansas. With armed confrontations between proslavery and antislavery settlers earning the state the moniker "Bleeding Kansas," reporters on the spot might have argued that the first shots of the Civil War did not take place at Sumter but rather in fights that included the Sack of Lawrence and the Battle of Osawatomie—fights that ultimately spilled east. Coverage of the fighting in Kansas came from reporters such as James Redpath, a correspondent for Greeley's *Tribune*. Among the stories that Redpath reported included the activities of militant abolitionist John Brown, who in Kansas had devised the Pottawatomie Massacre of proslavery settlers, making him both instantly notorious and indicative of the growing intensity with which abolitionists were willing to fight.

The Stakes of 1858

Beginning with the Panic of 1857—a failure in banks and businesses—the nation in 1858 had slid into a sharp economic recession, which in Illinois led to a halt in the construction of railroads and to a reduction in the money supply. In Chicago alone, more than 100 businesses failed, wiping out millions of dollars in investments.[17] Yet the dominant issue in the debates between Abraham Lincoln and Stephen A. Douglas in their bids for the Senate that year came from what had happened outside their state. While the fighting over what kind of constitution Kansans should adopt had become a national issue, the essence of each candidate's position in the debates revolved around their opposing interpretations of the role—past, present, and future—of slavery in the United States. Douglas argued on behalf of Popular Sovereignty, suggesting that both Whigs and Democrats had agreed to it in principle with the Compromise of 1850 and saying it was therefore fair to call it a national policy. Lincoln said that the national policy was to limit the spread of slavery, citing as an example the Northwest Ordinance of 1787 banning slavery from a large part of the modern-day Midwest.

Dating as far back as 1840, Lincoln and Douglas had already established a rivalry, when Lincoln, in support of William Henry Harrison's presidential campaign, had first debated the rising Democratic star. While they would compete again in the next presidential election, each as their respective party's nominee, their 1858 debates—a seminal moment in American political history featured two of the era's great orators debating issues of historic importance, with both men reflecting on the nation's past and suggesting opposing directions for its future.

Political debates were part of small-town culture in what would eventually become "the Midwest": they provided a source of entertainment for citizens, and the seven Lincoln-Douglas debates in August, September, and October 1858 represented some of the most highly anticipated and well-attended demonstrations of the type. Towns swelled well beyond their usual populations with attendees, and hotels, churches, and homes served as resting places for those who came from all over the state to witness the events.[18]

The candidates also engaged in partisan rhetoric, such as Douglas's accusations that Lincoln was a "Black Republican," a name for Republicans commonly used by the party's opponents who wished to associate members not only with abolitionists but also with slaves.[19] At first, Douglas's tactics put Lincoln on the defensive, but he countered with an attack on Douglas in Galesburg, Illinois: "I suppose that the real difference between Judge Douglas and his friends, and the Republicans on the contrary, is that the Judge is not in favor of making any difference between slavery and liberty," he said. "Judge Douglas declares that if any community wants slavery, they have a right to have it . . . but if you admit there is a wrong in it, he cannot logically say that anybody has a right to do wrong."[20]

Douglas said that even if a new state included slavery in its constitution, the local authorities could ignore such a law and that, without local enforcement by the police, slavery would not survive. Throughout the debates, Lincoln pressed Douglas on this question, expecting Douglas to explain how he could maintain his stance after having helped push the Kansas-Nebraska Act in the first place. The strategy came at the encouragement of Joseph Medill, editor of the *Chicago Tribune*, who had blasted Douglas as an opportunistic demagogue.[21]

However, strangely—especially for readers in Illinois—Republican newspapers in the East remained generally quiet about the events, troubling and later infuriating Lincoln's supporters, with Herndon complaining, "The East was for Douglas by silence."[22] A year before the debates, Douglas had thrilled eastern Republicans, including Weed, Seward, Greeley, and Raymond, in opposing President Buchanan over allowing Kansas to adopt the Lecompton Constitution, which essentially guaranteed the rights of slaveholders. When the Illinois senator maintained that the Buchanan administration had denied the people of Kansas the opportunity to vote in a legitimate election, even his harshest critics, Greeley among them, recognized Douglas's principled stand. Greeley even formed a coalition of midwestern Republicans to work toward convincing Douglas, known popularly as the "Little Giant," to join the Republican Party.[23]

Throughout the country, Greeley's admirers and critics alike understood that an endorsement from his *Tribune* lent tremendous support to whomever received it. So, when Republicans in Illinois learned that Greeley, a longtime friend and a nearly constant critic of the Democratic Party, had made statements supporting the Little Giant, they were shocked, knowing well that Lincoln's success to a certain extent depended on a New York endorsement. Greeley had written not only that Douglas's positions on the Lecompton vote had been correct but also that for holding them, he deserved another term in the Senate. In addition, to make matters even worse for Lincoln's faction, Greeley had counseled other Republican senators to support Douglas or face certain defeat in their own upcoming bids. Heeding Greeley's advice, a movement of Republicans for Douglas gathered momentum in the East.

Republicans in the West grew incensed with what they described as the tendencies of "Pharisaical old Whigs," namely Seward and Weed, who had promised to support Lincoln financially and politically but withdrew.[24] The ensuing silence from Greeley's *Tribune* about Lincoln's bid was even more troubling, as Greeley remained quiet about his reasoning.

Although they did not publicly say so, Greeley and other Republicans in the East had believed that Kansas would remain a problem for the next two years and that the Democrats would take the blame for it. In the end, or so they thought, the results would strengthen the Republicans' chances in other elections, including the upcoming presidential race. And although Greeley had since 1854 distanced himself from Seward and Weed, he insisted that his reasons for flirting with a Douglas endorsement were tied to a long-term strategy of ensuring a Republican presidency in 1860, which Seward would presumably win with Douglas's return to the Senate. Greeley had said to Lincoln's law partner William Herndon, who had opposed slavery even more staunchly than had the Illinois Senate candidate, "The Republican standard is too high. We want something practical."[25]

To a certain extent, Lincoln agreed with Greeley's position, and in attempts to modify the public's perception that he was a "Black Republican," he made statements that tempered the arguments he had made in the Douglas debates. "I am not, nor ever have been in favor of bringing about in any way the social and political equality of the white and black races," he said. "I am not, nor ever have been in favor of making voters or jurors of negroes, nor of qualifying them to hold office, or intermarry with white people; and I will say in addition to this that there is a physical difference between the white and black races which I believe will forever forbid the two races living together on terms of social and political equality. And inasmuch as they cannot so live, while they do remain together there must be the position of superior and inferior and I as much as any other man am in favor of having the superior position assigned to the white race."[26]

Regardless, the rift between the East and West among Republicans made apparent during the 1858 debates still stung Lincoln. For his part, Lincoln did what he could to look beyond the machinations. "I do not charge that G. [Greeley] was corrupt in this. I do not think he was, or is," he wrote his friend William Kellogg. "It was his judgment that the course he took was the best way of serving the Republican cause."[27] However, he also privately confided in Illinois senator Lyman Trumbull that he felt that Greeley sacrificed more than just a fellow Republican. "What does *The New York Tribune* mean by its constant eulogizing and admiring and magnifying Douglas?" Lincoln asked. "We would like to know it soon; it will save us a great deal of labor to surrender at once."[28] On another occasion, Lincoln complained to Herndon, "Greeley is not doing me right. His conduct, I believe, savors a little of injustice."[29] Chicago mayor and Lincoln supporter John Wentworth, a former Democrat, was much more incensed: "Our business is war, war, war on them!" he wrote in a letter to Lincoln, fearing that Seward, Weed, and "others of that school" had sold Lincoln's chances because they wanted "as little said about slavery as possible." He advised Lincoln to refocus his energies on the Republicans' next major contest, the 1860 presidential race.[30] Indeed, Lincoln did not give up his political aspirations and instead gave speeches to audiences outside of Illinois while his supporters began designs for his presidential nomination.

New York senator William H. Seward's designs on the presidency also became more apparent in October 1858, but with the delivery of his famous "Irrepressible Conflict" speech in Rochester, New York, southerners increasingly saw him—and the Republicans—as a threat not only to their legal rights but also to their very existence within the Union. Lincoln had delivered his "House Divided" speech four months before Seward's memorable address, and both described slavery in absolutist terms. The nation, Seward said, faced an "irrepressible conflict" between opposing and enduring forces, meaning the United States would sooner or later become either entirely a slaveholding nation or entirely free.[31] Lincoln had concurred, suggesting that a house divided could not stand—that the nation must be free or slave, but it could not continue on its present course. The speeches were met with expectedly split receptions, but most remarkably, southerners heard amid the talk of irrepressible division threats of war.

After tumultuous events at Harpers Ferry, Virginia, in October 1859, Lincoln, more compellingly than Seward, revisited the remarks both had made. In the year's final months, the nation was riveted by the trial of John Brown, who had reemerged as a national figure with another attack on slavery—this one even more sensational than his fights in Kansas. Brown had sought to start a slave insurrection with the takeover of the federal arsenal at Harpers Ferry, but the poorly planned attack resulted, at first, only in his capture, trial, and execution. By the time of his death, however, correspondents, editors, and readers nationally began reinterpreting the problems of regional differences, states' rights, and property—namely, slaves—with a newfound sense of urgency and, in some areas, panic.

The day after Brown's execution, Greeley's newspaper featured full coverage of the event with news and editorials, suggesting the epitaphs of Brown and his raiders would "remain unwritten until the not distant day when no slave shall clank his chains in the shades of Monticello, or by the graves of Mount Vernon."[32] In parts of the North, Brown reached martyrdom, with Reverend Theodore Parker describing him as a saint.[33] Such sentiments enraged the South, with the Alabama paper the *Montgomery Mail* calling for the execution of Greeley (who published Parker's letter), or at least the exile of the *Tribune* editor to an uninhabited island where beasts could prey on him.[34] In South Carolina, *Charleston Mercury* editor Robert Barnwell Rhett began publishing calls for secession.

Lincoln took the opportunity to speak about Brown's raid and the firestorm that had emerged from it in a speech he delivered at New York's Cooper Union in February 1860. The speech became one of his most important addresses, although it is not known as well as his classic statements at his inaugurations and at Gettysburg. (While Americans of Lincoln's day generally knew his 1860 speech as the "Cooper Institute" address, it has since become known as the Cooper Union address, after the name of the school that hosted lectures for the so-called People's Institute series.)[35] In the well-known conclusion to his speech, in which he insisted that "right makes might," he clarified the views he had expressed about slavery in the 1858 debates and affirmed he did not wish to see it expand into western territories, saying the Founders would have agreed with this position.[36] He then addressed accusations that Republicans were a sectional party that represented the interests only of the North and incited slave rebellions, dismissing allegations that the Republicans had backed Brown. "John Brown was no Republican," Lincoln said, "and you have failed to implicate a single Republican in his Harpers Ferry enterprise."[37]

The speech, much more than addressing the Brown controversy alone, marked quite possibly Lincoln's most famous pre-presidential appearance in public, not only galvanizing his support among those in the Midwest but also attracting an audience in the East, who looked to him for the first time as a serious contender for the Republican nomination. The event had drawn some of the most important political leaders in the country, with eighteen of them—from party leaders to the New York City police commissioner to lawyers and judges—seated on the stage with Lincoln. Three more attendees would join those on the stage: William Cullen Bryant, the progressive editor of the *Evening Post*; distinguished attorney David Dudley Field, with whom Lincoln had shared the stage at the Chicago River and Harbor Convention; and Greeley, who had until then quietly headed the movement of those determined to dump Seward as the favored Republican candidate. The final portion of the speech encouraged Republicans to use reason in their actions and called upon his audience to "let us, to the end, dare to do our duty as we understand it." Politically, the event raised his stature in the East, with Henry Raymond's *Times*, among others, printing the speech in its entirety on the front page and describing Lincoln as a leader of preeminent ability.[38]

Lincoln knew any success in a campaign for president would depend on an impressive performance during the event. Republicans who looked beyond regional interests or the appeal of individual candidates also recognized the event as an important one if they were to secure a national strategy with a successful outcome in November. If Lincoln the westerner could capture support in the East, as both his Illinois supporters and the group of Greeley-led Republicans in the East reasoned, he would undoubtedly succeed in the West with the popular vote and likely carry the election. However, a candidate from New York, the same strategists deduced, would most likely not gain enough support in the West to offset sure losses in southern border states, where an eastern Republican would stand no chance at all.[39]

One of Lincoln's most enthusiastic supporters after the event was Greeley, who not only served as a witness to the speech but also published it in the *Tribune* the next day. Attending the address as one of the leading audience members on the stage, Greeley had the opportunity to close the event by giving a short speech of his own. Reconsidering the decision he had made to withhold support for Lincoln in his 1858 bid for the Senate, Greeley said the rising Republican of the West had provided an example of what free labor and the free expression of ideas could produce. The next morning after the address, the *Tribune* praised Lincoln's speech as "one of the happiest and most convincing political arguments ever made."[40]

As Lincoln's political capital ascended sharply in New York, Weed, still a venerable force in national politics, was determined to launch a Seward candidacy. In the winter of 1859–60, he had developed a scheme to furnish, through the New York legislature, charters for city railroads, whose grantees were in turn to supply several hundred thousand dollars for the Republicans—from which Seward would directly benefit in his presidential campaign. Greeley's old associates presumed they could rely on the *Tribune* to support Seward's campaign, if for no other reason than because all three were New Yorkers (along with the fact that they had worked with Greeley on previous campaigns). Weed and Seward had apparently forgotten the caustic letter they had received from Greeley in 1854, dissolving his ties from "the firm"; Greeley, of course, had not.

Splitting Rails

Leading up to the 1860 Republican convention in Chicago, the loyalties of the *Chicago Tribune* to Lincoln remained unquestioned, with editors Joseph Medill and Charles Henry Ray describing him, not Seward, as the nation's premier spokesperson. Lincoln used "no tricks of oratory, nothing for mere stage effect, but inspired by the grandeur of his theme," and, the Chicago newspaper suggested, "the Republican Party, and indeed, the whole American people, have reason to be proud of Abraham Lincoln."[41]

The Democrats held their convention first, meeting in April 1860 in Charleston, South Carolina. Northern and southern delegates split over the issue of slavery and, not being able to agree upon a candidate, had to reconvene. In Baltimore, Maryland, northern Democrats agreed to support Lincoln's old rival, Stephen A. Douglas; however, southern Democrats protested and, in a third convention, met to nominate their own candidate, John C. Breckinridge of Kentucky. Compounding the split among southern Democrats, former senator John Bell of Tennessee headed the splinter Constitutional Union Party in an attempt to represent the border states and the ideals of compromise found in the deceased Whig Party.

The Republicans opened proceedings May 16, 1860, with the most remarkable events of the first day, from many accounts, surrounding the presence of Greeley. Weed had arranged tight control over the selection of New York delegates, who were expected to help launch Seward's nomination quickly and successfully, and Greeley, having distanced himself from both Weed and Seward, had stood no chance of serving as a New York delegate. But by chance, fortune, or Greeley's own maneuverings (to this day, the logistics of the arrangement are still not clear), Greeley had received a proxy appointment to attend the convention from an absentee Oregon delegate.[42]

Oregon's geographic distance from the convention had worked to Greeley's favor. Because of a change in the planned date of the convention, which organizers had originally scheduled for June, and because of Oregon's remote location, the Republicans of that state received word of the rescheduling much later than delegates in states farther east. Scrambling to put together a delegation of representatives who could both afford the time and expense necessary for the trip to Chicago, the Oregon party selected proxies to represent them, one of whom included the well-known Republican advocate and head of the *New York Tribune*.[43]

Greeley's presence in Chicago was not at all coincidental or without consequence. In fact, the platform eventually developed by the Republicans reflected revisions and content contributed directly by Greeley. While he earned critics for deleting strong antislavery language from it, which he described as "needlessly offensive or irritating," his efforts, in the end, secured a message that unified the North.[44] Moreover, in turning his support to Lincoln, Greeley, after arriving in Chicago, provided the Illinoisan a necessary boost in the nomination process, arguably one that Lincoln needed to ensure the presidency.

With Greeley's unexpected arrival in Chicago, rumors began to swirl that there had been a break in the New York delegation, which, it had been assumed until the convention, would easily secure Seward's nomination. While Lincoln's operatives worked quietly behind the scenes, enthusiastic Seward supporters crowded the streets and hotels of Chicago. Flyers stoking the New York divisions flooded the city streets with the simple announcement, "Greeley at the Tremont: Weed at the Richmond House," insinuating that the two were no longer working directly together. The split struck many Republicans in Chicago as news, primarily because few had heard (or had cared) about Greeley's otherwise confidential split from Seward and Weed in 1854. Still, few entertained thoughts that Lincoln would defeat Seward. Even Greeley, who had already publicly announced his support for conservative Edward Bates of Missouri, had telegraphed the *Tribune* office in New York that "the opposition to Governor Seward cannot be concentrated on any other candidate" and that readers could expect to read about Seward's forthcoming candidacy.[45]

Lincoln's supporters—at the Tremont House also—had set up their convention headquarters five blocks from the convention site. While Lincoln stayed close to his home in Springfield, Illinois, monitoring updates from Chicago at the city's telegraph office, his operatives on the convention floor worked quietly on his behalf, having resolved in the week before the election to make their candidate not only the next nominee but also the next president. On May 10, 1860, the Republicans of Illinois had met in Decatur to consolidate their support and develop a strategy for the upcoming national convention. In one of the most famous campaign stunts in American political history, Richard J. Oglesby, a vigorous young politician from Decatur, had consulted with John Hanks, an elderly first cousin of Lincoln's mother, and located two rails from a fence Lincoln was said to have erected in 1830. On the first day of the meeting, Oglesby organized a display of the rails adorned with labels advertising them as split by Lincoln himself. "Honest Abe" could not pass up the opportunity for self-promotion. "It is true I helped build a house for my father," he said. "Whether these are some of the identical rails I cannot say. Quite likely they are."[46]

In Chicago, Oglesby and Herndon, along with David Davis, Stephen T. Logan, Leonard Swett, Norman Judd, Jesse K. Dubois, associates and friends Lincoln had made during his years in politics and as a lawyer, all worked the floor to dicker for votes on behalf of their candidate. Among their first successes, they helped to secure the support of Greeley, who at first favored only "anybody to beat Seward," but with Herndon's persuasion, Greeley threw his influence to Lincoln. Another recruit, a Dr. Ames, was a Democrat and not a resident of Chicago, but the group contacted him via telegraph and called him to take the first train to the city. Ames was instructed to organize two groups of men who had all developed reputations for having extraordinarily loud voices. These men would find appropriate locations on opposite sides of the convention hall that would maximize the volume of their shouts and bellows. With the signal of a waving handkerchief in the hands of a Lincoln man on the platform, the men were to emit yells that would raise the roof of the hall. The signals were frequently given, and the response was so effective that not only did the tide of support swing to Lincoln but Ames, it was said, became so enthralled with the shouting that he joined the Republican Party and later received his reward with the appointment to a postmaster position.[47]

Lincoln had begun his bid for the nomination with a new image—not one of a country bumpkin or a small-town lawyer but as a strong and honest frontiersman. At the end of the first day, his chances still appeared slim, with the first round of voting indicating that Seward indeed led in the delegate count. However, Seward had not managed to secure the margin necessary for the nomination, and with Pennsylvania senator Simon Cameron winning a substantial number of ballots for third place (Seward 173.5; Lincoln 102; Cameron 50.5), Lincoln's success depended on Pennsylvania. In the words of William Butler, a longtime friend of Lincoln's who came to his aid during the convention by providing updates from the convention floor, the rift among eastern Republicans had grown beyond the rumor stage. "The strife between dilegates [*sic*] from New York & Pennsylvania still rage [*sic*] high," he wrote at the close of the first day. "Pennsylvania will never go for Seward."[48]

Dubois, who had served with Lincoln in the state legislature, telegraphed the candidate with an update that his supporters had nearly secured the votes of Pennsylvania delegates, but they needed to offer Cameron a position in the cabinet in order to do so. "I authorize no bargains and will be bound by none," Lincoln replied. However, not content with the possible loss of Pennsylvania support, Lincoln sent a copy of the *Missouri Democrat* to Herndon with notes he wrote in the margins of Seward's speech transcriptions. "I agree with Seward's 'irrepressible conflict,' but do not agree with his 'higher law' doctrine," he had written. "Make no contracts that will bind me."[49]

It was on the second day that Lincoln's supporters, who now included Greeley, began their moves. Greeley, who later downplayed his role in the Bates campaign, began lobbying on the convention floor against Seward, who, he told delegates (especially those from Pennsylvania and Indiana), would be easily corrupted. When Cameron dropped out after the second ballot and threw his support to Lincoln, the difference narrowed to Seward with 184.5 to Lincoln's 181. Butler followed with another update: "Your friends are doing all that can be done for you," he wrote, including encouraging news that Chicago mayor John Wentworth, who had converted from the Democratic Party to the Republicans, had also lent his support, offering to help cover the costs of the convention.[50]

In light of Lincoln's gains with the second round of voting, the role of players at the Chicago convention—from Oglesby, Butler, and Wentworth to Seward, Weed, and Greeley—subsequently became the subject of historical debate. Although historians recognize primarily the contributions of Lincoln's supporters in Illinois, Greeley's role in the final vote cannot be underestimated, with Weed's account of a seemingly innocuous encounter between Greeley and an old friend of Weed's—Julius Wood of Columbus, Ohio—in hindsight containing an exchange of critical importance to the outcome of the final vote. "We shan't nominate Seward," Greeley had said to Wood months before the convention: "[W]e'll take some more conservative man, like Pitt Fessenden or Bates"—or, as it turned out under the circumstances, Lincoln. According to Weed, Wood told Seward, "Greeley is cheating you. He will go to Chicago and work against you." Seward responded: "My dear Wood . . . your zeal sometimes gets a little the better of your judgment."[51]

The next vote on the floor of the Chicago convention—the third and final one—proved determinative. With the exposure of Weed's plans for lucrative New York railroad contracts, the delegates of Indiana also turned to Lincoln, whose numbers had risen to 231.5 votes to Seward's 180. With 233 votes required for the nomination, Lincoln's supporters rushed to find delegates from Maryland, Kentucky, and Virginia who might still be swayed to support him.

The final tally, as Greeley described it, included votes that were rapidly transferred to Lincoln until he had 354 of the 466 possible, locking the nomination.[52] Greeley was, of course, thrilled: his plan to usurp Seward had succeeded. While Lincoln's supporters had even more reason to celebrate, their reaction reverberated, in Herndon's words, from coast to coast. Upon word of the final vote, "the cannon planted on the roof of the Wigwam [the convention hall] belched forth a boom across the Illinois prairies," he wrote. "The sound was taken up and reverberated from Maine to California. With the nomination of Hannibal Hamlin [for vice president], of Maine, the convention adjourned. The delegates—victorious and vanquished alike—turned their steps homeward, and the great campaign of 1860 had begun."[53]

Joy at the convention was not universal. When Weed learned of Seward's defeat, he reportedly broke down in tears, claiming he had been unaware that Greeley had harbored any ill feelings about his partner from previous campaigns. Seeing no mistake in the way he had managed Seward's campaign, Weed called on Raymond's *Times*, his most reliable supporter in the New York press, and both blamed Greeley for the misfortune. Raymond began running accounts in the *Times* of the events in Chicago that cast Greeley in an unflattering light. Announcing what had taken place in 1854—although it had seemed innocuous at the time—he declared that Greeley was "deliberately wreaking the long-hoarded revenge of a disappointed office-seeker."[54] There was truth to the allegation, as Greeley's 1854 letter had complained bitterly that Seward and Weed had tried to humiliate him by nominating Henry Raymond for the role of lieutenant governor. "No other name could have been put upon the ticket so bitterly humbling to me," Greeley had written, "as that which was selected."[55]

Greeley responded to accusations of having engaged in petty personal politics by giving a speech just a few days after the convention, saying, "The past is dead. Let the dead past bury it, and let its mourners, if they will, go about the streets." Weed responded bitterly: "The 'mourners,' to whom Mr. Greeley alludes . . . constitute the rank and file, as well as the intelligence and patriotism of nearly every Republican state in the Union."[56] The *Times*, in response, claimed Seward would have undoubtedly won the nomination had Greeley not exploited the apprehensions of delegates from Pennsylvania and Indiana in particular. In June 1860, Raymond more fully embarrassed Greeley by calling on him to publish the letter he had written Seward in 1854.[57] After first resisting, Greeley bowed to public pressure and published the letter in the *Tribune*, hoping to put the matter to rest.

Seward's supporters, who had expected to campaign for him through Election Day in November, had already printed thousands of pamphlets and circulars—all ready for distribution as soon as word of the nomination had arrived. Reflecting on Seward's loss, one description of the outcome cast the materials as lying hopelessly idle and in piles, "rendered a dead and cumbrous mass of useless material, unfit for any but one purpose."[58] Seward, for his part, met the news about his defeat as well as could be expected, agreeing to the request of Republicans to issue a statement of support for Lincoln. However, in efforts to make the Republicans appear divided still, at least a few Democratic newspapers in the North either downplayed the speech or ignored it entirely, presenting to Seward the necessity of writing Lincoln directly. He included a copy of the speech from the *New York Times* as evidence that he had fulfilled expectations, assuring Lincoln he was confident his backers in New York would respond accordingly and, in November, support the candidate from Illinois.[59]

A FIGHT FOR UNION AND FOR FREEDOM

I n the months following Abraham Lincoln's presidential nomination at the Chicago convention, publishers scrambled to find information about him for a voting public that knew little about the Republican candidate from Illinois. Among the most informative of the thirteen Lincoln campaign biographies that appeared in 1860 included one compiled by John Locke Scripps, a friend of Lincoln's and an editor of and shareholder in the *Chicago Tribune*. Lincoln had prepared an autobiographical sketch for Scripps, and although it was brief, it provided more information on his political background than did an autobiography he had drafted in 1859. Knowing a hard stand on the slavery issue might repel potential supporters, Lincoln made few comments on it, other than to reproduce a denunciation that he had made more than twenty years before as "injustice and bad policy." However, he did address with more detail the stand he had taken in the House against the Mexican-American War, knowing his opponents would attempt to hold his past positions against him.[1]

Lincoln and his primary opponent, Democratic nominee Stephen A. Douglas, had both made clear their insistence that the Union must hold and that, despite recurring threats from southern states throughout the latter part of 1860, disunion was simply not an option. Douglas made speeches throughout the South, trying to emphasize his differences with Lincoln, but he nonetheless insisted that no grievance could justify secession. Yet, as Douglas continued to campaign, southern editors published an address by Jefferson Davis that pushed for secession if the results from Democratic states in the fall election made it necessary.

As the campaign for "Honest Old Abe" swung into full operation with the support of both the Chicago and New York Republican machinery, a myriad of Lincoln portraits became available on ornaments and paraphernalia. With his homespun (and homely) profile also appearing in print materials, including pamphlets and newspapers, in which people read the story of his humble beginnings, Lincoln began to relive a history he had helped to create exactly twenty years earlier. Lincoln "The Rail Splitter" had replaced Harrison "the Log-Cabin Candidate," at times with virtually identical imagery. However, a notable difference during the 1860 campaign included the seriousness of Lincoln's organizers. "It was the revived spirit of the Harrison campaign," William Herndon wrote, "shorn of its fun and frolic [and] strengthened by the power of organization and the tremendous impetus of earnest devotion to a high principle."[2]

Horace Greeley's response to Lincoln's campaign exceeded the efforts he had invested in securing his nomination, and following the Chicago convention, the *New York Tribune* featured stories and editorials with enthusiastic support for Lincoln and the Republican ticket. A report from the Republican Central Campaign Club published in the *Tribune* claimed Lincoln's popularity would allow him to sweep states "like a tornado" and "run like chain lightning from the Allegheny to the Missouri."[3] Such content also boosted circulation of the *Tribune* throughout the Midwest, bringing its combined daily and weekly totals to 300,000—by Election Day, the daily edition alone reached 72,500 copies, with the demand for election returns boosting sales to the unprecedented number.[4]

However, Greeley was only half-correct in his assessment of the nation's mood. While Republicans did indeed rally behind Lincoln after the Chicago convention, the Democratic Party remained split. Although under ordinary circumstances, such a division might have simply worked toward the advantage of the Republicans, the 1860 election was no ordinary event. With an electorate entrenched in factions, Stephen Douglas (the northern Democrat), John Breckinridge (the southern Democrat), and John Bell (of the Constitutional

Union Party) battled for support in parts of the country where voters feared outright the rise of the Republicans. The fragmented canvas gave secessionists in the summer of 1860 reason to entertain the possibility that the House might have to decide the election, as it appeared possible that no one candidate might secure the required electoral majority. Therefore, a disputed election could either give secessionists grounds, they reasoned, to question the integrity of the results—and, ultimately, of the Union itself—or provide the opportunity to put a southern rights advocate into the White House instead of a Republican. The remaining option, previously described only in the fiery rhetoric of abolitionists and secessionists alike, was the otherwise inconceivable route of war.

Instead of letting divisive interests derail the November election, Greeley published the leading documents associated with them in the form of *A Political Text-Book for 1860*. The text, which became one of the Lincoln campaign's leading pieces of promotional literature, gave voice to Republicans as well as to proslavery advocates, abolitionists, northern Democrats, and secessionists alike. The *Tribune* ran front-page ads for the 250-page item, declaring that every politician and every political club should have a copy, which sold for one dollar.[5] It provided readers with an educational summary of the presidential nomination and election process, the national platforms adopted by the four parties, and speeches and letters from Bell, Breckinridge, Douglas, and Lincoln, among others, citing almanac-like figures, which included the returns of all presidential elections since 1836. Most important, it featured abbreviated histories of the struggle to end slavery and of the action of Congress regarding the freedom of public lands—two issues Lincoln and Greeley had made synonymous with their experiences as legislators in the late 1840s.

Despite conventional wisdom, Greeley even targeted southern voters, who (for the most part) feared a Republican presidency as the worst of all possible election results.[6] The *Tribune* even published letters allegedly submitted by "friends in the Slave States" who had asked, "For whom shall we cast our votes, seeing that we are not at liberty to vote for Lincoln and Hamlin?" Greeley's advice to them was not to vote at all if they could not vote according to free convictions.

"But (in many, if not most cases) you can vote for Lincoln—you will if you have but manly courage," he wrote. "If you know any voters of like faith with yourselves, agree beforehand with them on the hour at which you will together go quietly to the polls and offer your votes for Lincoln Electors: if they are refused, or if they are accepted and then destroyed or not returned, your duty is performed."[7]

On Election Day, "Honest Abe" was indeed elected the sixteenth president of the United States, carrying an electoral majority but with only 40 percent of the vote. Voting for the Republican's "Rail-Splitter Candidate" was not even an option in half of the country, as Lincoln's name did not appear on ballots in southern states. Votes elsewhere illustrated the national split: just as Lincoln won the northern part of his home state and lost to Douglas in southern Illinois, he won much of the state of New York but lost New York City. In Manhattan in particular, despite Greeley's efforts, urban laborers feared the prospect of a Republican in the White House in part because of allegations published by pro-Democratic newspapers—specifically, that Lincoln would force them to compete for jobs with "four million emancipated negroes."[8]

The Trouble with Uncle Horace

The night after the election, in a show of appreciation for Greeley's efforts to promote the Lincoln campaign, Republicans asked Greeley to speak at a victory rally at New York's Stuyvesant Institute. Greeley and thousands of revelers were satisfied that the new administration would bring, in his words, a renewed appreciation for "all great, just, and true expositions of the law of righteousness and freedom." With the praise he had showered upon Henry Clay in eulogies to the Whig icon now a distant memory, Greeley said he was proud the election proved that the Republicans were "not a man-worshiping party"—a statement he could afford to make because, at the time of his speech, he enjoyed greater popularity in New York City than Lincoln did.[9] Far from the assessments of the most optimistic Republicans, however, the events that followed revealed, in Lincoln's words, a condition of the national spirit that was "not what either party, or any man devised, or expected."[10]

Meanwhile, the leading Democratic newspapers of New York, which had helped to sway the vote against Lincoln in urban areas, coalesced in recognizing him as the Union president. Few—unlike their counterparts in the South—dared call upon readers to join the rebellion. Even *New York Herald* editor James Gordon Bennett, who generally supported Democratic candidates, provided the president with unlikely support, suggesting that Lincoln ought to reward Greeley with a cabinet appointment for his role in securing the new administration's rise to power. It would have made perfect business sense for Bennett to hope Greeley would leave his editorial post, removing him as the *Herald*'s most formidable competitor, but Bennett's record during Lincoln's presidency also revealed his dedication to the Union.[11]

Unsurprisingly, letters from Greeley's friends recommending him for office arrived in Lincoln's mail. John W. Forney, a Pennsylvania editor, encouraged Lincoln to find an appointment for Greeley primarily because a wide audience, from the Northeast to the Midwest, read and admired the *Tribune*. Greeley's influence on the masses, Forney wrote, made him an ideal candidate for federal office, as Greeley was "the first journalist in America"—a populist "entitled to the thanks of his party" for his vigor, courage, and integrity.[12]

Throughout his first term as president and as late as April 1865, Lincoln apparently did entertain the possibility of appointing Greeley to his administration. But during the presidential campaign of 1864, Lincoln—with recollections of the Chicago convention hardly part of a distant past—explained to a New York lawyer and supporter why he had not and could not appoint Greeley to the cabinet: the answer was William H. Seward. The two New Yorkers, who had long since abandoned a professional relationship and had replaced it with cold non-recognition for each other, would create intolerable conditions, Lincoln reasoned. However, Lincoln had said that if Greeley were to have a role, he would have appointed him to the postmaster general position, a role that the editor had sought for much of his professional life. "Do you know, I believe Greeley would make a good Postmaster General," Lincoln said. "I think I am right in saying that this is the position he would rather occupy than any other."[13]

Over the past decade, Lincoln and Greeley had developed generally compatible, albeit sometimes tense, relationships with allies com-
mitted to the ideals of the Republican Party. However, when Lincoln
appointed Seward secretary of state and left the *Tribune* editor to tend
to his newspaper, Greeley took the gesture as an insult. Instead of
continuing to support Lincoln as he had done since the Republican
convention, Greeley responded by using the *Tribune* to support the
president's war policy but also to hector the president personally.

More immediately, Greeley's remedy was to seek the Senate seat
vacated by Seward in a campaign supported primarily by the content
of his own *Tribune*. He styled himself as the Republican candidate
and sought backing from those whom he had helped in the past.
But Lincoln, upon hearing from Thurlow Weed of Greeley's designs,
disavowed an endorsement. Although he thought well of Greeley,
Lincoln wrote in a letter to Weed, he made clear the president's
name "*must* not be used in the Senatorial election, in favor of, or
against anyone" (Lincoln's emphasis).[14] In an ironic reversal of past
events, Weed arranged for Ira Harris, a jurist, to enter the race as a
Republican. Greeley almost won his bid, but the legislature instead
chose Harris to replace Seward, for the moment allowing Weed to
avenge the results of Chicago. And although "Uncle Horace," as he
was affectionately known among readers, maintained a loyal following for the inspired content of his newspaper, his colleagues in the
press came to regard him as unreliable and even detrimental to the
conservative ideals of Union promoted by Lincoln.

History may have since forgotten that Horace Greeley, at least
in the minds of his audience, took the lead in popularizing the idea
that the Civil War should become a fight to free all men. Part of
the problem with this legacy stems from Greeley's own actions, as
almost immediately after Lincoln's election and until his assassination, opinions published in the *Tribune*—whether Greeley's or his
editors'—vacillated. In November 1860, for example, Greeley at first
had given readers the impression that the North should not take the
threats of secessionists seriously. "If South Carolina shall be left to
stand alone, we think she must ultimately recede," read one editorial.[15] "But if ever seven or eight States send agents to Washington

to say 'We want to get out of the Union,'" read another, "we shall feel constrained by our devotion to Human Liberty to say, 'Let them go!'"[16] But after Lincoln's inauguration, a famous series of *Tribune* editorials then called upon the president and the nation to "Stand Firm" in preserving the Union and to defeat secessionists with military force if necessary.[17]

"What in the world is the matter with Uncle Horace?" Lincoln would ask at one point during the ensuing war. "Why can't he restrain himself and wait a little?"[18] Compelled to respond to Greeley's call, Lincoln summoned governors from Indiana, Maine, Illinois, Wisconsin, Michigan, and Ohio to Washington, D.C., on April 6, 1861, to build a hard line against secession. But in the meantime, the gulf between North and South had grown so vast that few in the North, including Lincoln, understood that words such as those written by Greeley had struck secessionists as grounds for war. *New York Times* editor Henry Raymond had astutely sensed the direction in which the nation had turned and had counseled Lincoln on the steps he should take to avoid conflict, urging the president to assuage southern fears. Perhaps because he had no other option, Lincoln rebuffed the appeal and framed the misunderstanding in the South as one that would go away.[19] Over the next four years, the war would prove Lincoln's initial determinations wrong.

The Nation's War Cry

As it became clear that beliefs in a peaceable dissolution of the Union were hopeless, Greeley, of all editors in the North, stood to lose prestige because of his contradictory statements that Lincoln could both suppress the rebellion and avoid war. As South Carolina led the movement toward dissolving the Union, other states followed. With the firing of the first shots of the Civil War on April 12, 1861, Greeley—or at least the *Tribune*'s policy—again changed course: "Sumter is temporarily lost, but Freedom is saved!" he wrote. He called on northerners to unite for the Union, writing, "It is hard to lose Sumter, but in losing it we have gained a united people. Long live the Republic."[20] And from June 26 to July 4, 1861, the *Tribune* then ran a series of columns, "The Nation's War-Cry," urging Lincoln to send federal troops into Virginia to capture the Confederate capital of Richmond.[21]

Greeley was away from the newspaper in late July, having left managing editor Charles A. Dana in charge. Fitz-Henry Warren, the *Tribune*'s Washington correspondent, wrote much of the *Tribune*'s most belligerent material immediately before the first major conflict of the war, later called the First Battle of Bull Run, also known as Manassas, in Virginia. However, Greeley's conscience was burdened with news of the rout of the Union Army, a fight that was attributed, at least in part, to his newspaper's role in pressuring Lincoln to fight. The outcome of such pressure was a fiasco for the Union known as the "Great Skedaddle" in which thousands of unprepared troops fled the battlefield. Reports published in his own newspaper startled even Greeley. "The strange and disastrous retreat of our troops from their well-contested position at Bull's Run to their old quarters at Arlington yesterday formed the topic of much gloomy conversation and somber conjecture," the *Tribune* reported. "It was only when the fighting was done, and the ridiculous panic turned the heads of the men, that they seemed to waver."[22]

Indeed, Greeley also panicked at the news, suffering a nervous breakdown once the bloodiness of the battle, which levied thousands of casualties, became evident. Forced to apologize to his audience for the *Tribune*'s martial fervor before Bull Run, he blamed at least part of the content on Dana and, at the same time, hurriedly defended the *Tribune* to readers shocked by the results. "I am charged with what is called 'opposing the administration' because of that selection, and various paragraphs which have from time to time appeared in the *Tribune* are quoted to sustain this inculpation," he wrote. "If I am needed as a scapegoat for all the military blunders of the last month, so be it. Individuals must die that the nation may live. If I can serve her best in that capacity, I do not shrink from the ordeal."[23]

With Greeley acknowledging that the results of the battle had made him "all but insane," he wrote Lincoln shortly after his public apology, privately urging him to surrender.[24] The letter included frenetic language that reflected his mental state. "This is my seventh sleepless night—yours, too, doubtless—yet I think I shall not die, because I have no right to die. I must struggle to live, however bitterly," he wrote. "You are not considered a great man, and I am a hopelessly broken one. You are now undergoing a terrible ordeal, and God has thrown the gravest responsibility upon you. Do not fear to meet them." A transcription of this remarkable letter, available through the Library of Congress, includes the emphases and editing in Greeley's original, tortured handwriting, closing with the suggestion: "'Whoso would lose his life for my sake shall save it,' do the thing that is the highest right, and tell me how I am to second you."[25]

Lincoln, with supreme patience, hid the letter for three years before quietly disclosing its contents in a private conversation with his secretaries John G. Nicolay and John Hay. Nicolay had remarked that the *New York Herald*'s editor, James Gordon Bennett, would probably pay $10,000 for the letter, but Lincoln replied, "I need $10,000 very much, but he could not have it for many times that."[26] However, Lincoln did complain publicly after Bull Run that Greeley specifically, over a related matter, had treated him poorly. In a speech, he cited a *Tribune* editorial that criticized Union regiments at Bull Run—after waving the truce flag, they allegedly began burying troops while watching Confederate soldiers seize blacks who helped with the burials, sending them back into slavery. "Horace Greeley said in his paper," Lincoln protested, "that the government would probably do nothing about it. What *could* I do?" (Lincoln's emphasis).[27]

Regardless, looking beyond immediate circumstances, Lincoln considered Greeley an ally and maintained respect for the editor, who in many ways helped articulate in writing what Lincoln could say generally to much smaller audiences. When Greeley was scheduled to speak in a lecture series at Washington's Smithsonian Institute, Lincoln arranged to attend. Greeley's speech would focus on the reasons why the president needed to make abolition a chief goal of the war. Knowing in advance the subject of the evening, Lincoln had said to his advisors, "In print, every one of his words seems to weigh about a ton. I want to see what he has to say about this."[28] Lincoln not only attended the lecture but also sat on the stage while Greeley delivered it, and although Greeley's calls for abolition clearly resonated with the president's own long-term interests, managing both the war and the efforts of editors in the North, including Greeley, would make emancipation an epic endeavor.

In measures still considered controversial, Lincoln did respond to the press shortly after the beginning of the war by suspending the writ of habeas corpus and allowing for the prosecution of newspapermen for publishing content that jeopardized Union war efforts.[29] Greeley and other members of the press, whether seeking to protect their rights or simply to attract readers, had published sensitive military operations and, in doing so, had infuriated the president's generals by allowing Confederate leaders to anticipate Union troop movements. On one such occasion, the *Tribune* revealed the plans of General William Tecumseh Sherman, who had prepared to attack either Charlotte or Raleigh, North Carolina, resulting in a battle lost for the Union. "If I could have caught Mr. Greeley during the war," Sherman wrote, "I would have hung him."[30]

For these reasons, and due to the inexcusable failures of Union generals, the opening year of the war went disastrously for the North, and it was clear that Lincoln would need to reconsider his strategy for preserving the Union. Abolitionists had pressured Lincoln to end slavery almost immediately after he had assumed the presidency, believing first and foremost that it was the right thing to do but also, as the war progressed, that it would demoralize the South and contribute to Union victory. While Lincoln approved of the principle of abolition, he did not see his power as president as including the role of ending slavery, postponing action on the matter until he believed it had obtained wider public support. Regardless, the president had held a deep-seated hatred for slavery his entire life, and at one point, later in the war, the felt the need to defend the stance. In a letter to Kentucky editor A. G. Hodges, he wrote that if slavery was not wrong, nothing was wrong. "And yet I have never understood that the Presidency conferred upon me an unrestricted right to act officially upon this judgment and feeling. It was in the oath I took, that I would to the best of my ability preserve, protect, and defend the Constitution of the United States."[31]

The New Birth of Freedom

Since his days in Congress, Lincoln had supported the Wilmot Proviso as a way to constrict the spread of slavery, and on June 19, 1862, he signed legislation that prohibited the practice in the territories, accomplishing at least part of what Representative David Wilmot had first proposed in 1846. At the same time, the president's stance on the role that slavery would play in the war also changed with the course of the war itself. In March 1862, he wrote Greeley, indicating that he was again considering abolishing slavery in Washington, D.C., a ban that he would sign into effect three weeks later. But, just as he had been unsure about the implications of such a measure when he had entertained it as a Whig in Congress, he wrote that as president, he felt "uneasy" about "the time and manner of doing it."[32]

Although the ban on slavery in the District would not come for another year, Congress in July 1862 passed the Second Confiscation Act, which allowed for the freeing of slaves belonging to everyone in rebellion against the government. The legislation provided the signal desired among abolitionists, who further called on Lincoln to enforce the change and demonstrate an increased intolerance for the institution. However, Lincoln—the visionary—had already drafted what he termed the Preliminary Proclamation, the first version of the Emancipation Proclamation, and he read an initial draft of it to William H. Seward, secretary of state, and Gideon Welles, secretary of the navy, on July 13, 1862. Hearing the language of what would become the Emancipation Proclamation at first rendered both secretaries speechless. Seward feared the measure would appear to the Confederate States as a sign of desperation and trigger an insurrection in the North among those who did not support abolition, and when Lincoln found Welles apparently too confused to respond, he temporarily let the matter drop.[33]

Taken at face value, the Emancipation Proclamation was the most revolutionary pronouncement ever signed by an American president.[34] It would strike the legal shackles from four million black slaves and set the nation's face toward the total abolition of slavery within three more years. While Seward in particular had seen the need for the president to act judiciously in presenting the measure to the public, Lincoln, later in July, again raised the issue of emancipation in a regularly scheduled cabinet meeting. This time, it was met with a mixed reaction. While Lincoln had wanted the advice of his advisors only on the style of the proclamation and not on its substance, they had a good deal to say about both. Secretary of War Edwin M. Stanton advocated its immediate release, correctly interpreting the measure as one that would both deprive the Confederacy of slave labor and bring additional men into the Union Army. Treasury Secretary Salmon P. Chase also supported it, but Postmaster General Montgomery Blair foresaw defeat in the fall elections. Attorney General Edward Bates, a conservative, opposed equality for blacks but gave his qualified support.

Soon thereafter, an exchange took place between Lincoln and Greeley, one that was less coincidental than it was indicative of the times. The exchange was also one of the most famous examples of what was known during the era as "personal journalism," a practice somewhat peculiar during the Civil War to major editors who sought to shape and direct public opinion by the force of their reputations alone. In an editorial titled "The Prayer of Twenty Millions," Greeley used the *Tribune* to call upon Lincoln to wage war against the South in the name of ending slavery.[35] The twenty million to whom Greeley referred were northern workers who had labored tirelessly on behalf of a cause—bringing the South back to the Union—that they could no longer support. On August 20, 1862, Greeley published the "Prayer," which complained that the Union had suffered immensely from the president's deference to rebel slavery and urged Lincoln to use the Second Confiscation Act to free the slaves of rebel masters.[36]

Remarkably, Lincoln chose to reply to Greeley by publishing a letter in the *National Intelligencer*, whose editors were pro-Union but not staunch supporters of the president and decidedly against emancipation. The substance of what Lincoln wrote indicated that he continued to believe that his first task was to preserve the Union. "My paramount object in this struggle is to save the Union, and is not either to save or destroy slavery," he wrote. "If I could save the Union without freeing any slave, I would do it, and if I could save it by freeing all the slaves, I would do it; and if I could save it by freeing some and leaving others alone, I would also do that."[37] In this case, having already decided privately to issue the Emancipation Proclamation, Lincoln's immediate public response did not reflect his discussions with his cabinet, which included his plans to link "partial" emancipation with the salvation of the Union. Lincoln later explained to a *Tribune* correspondent that he intended the letter to Greeley to explain to the public that he would not declare emancipation until the measure received wider support throughout the North.[38]

While Greeley deserves credit for raising the issue of abolition to one that the public would recognize as an important aspect of the war, Lincoln deserves credit for understanding the importance of managing not only information but editors as well. According to biographer Allen Guelzo, the events surrounding the release of the Emancipation Proclamation demonstrated Lincoln's skills in anticipating the likely responses of Greeley's *Tribune* in particular. Knowing that even the hint of abolition would trigger widespread reaction in the press, Lincoln arranged to have the news of administrative action leaked by inviting one of Greeley's writers, journalist James R. Gilmore, to a meeting on August 18. Lincoln suggested to Gilmore that it was all right for him to mention the impending announcement about the Emancipation Proclamation to his boss, which in itself, Guelzo notes, may have triggered Greeley's "Prayer," amounting to a demand for the president to make public what he had cleverly disclosed in private to Gilmore.[39]

In a number of respects, Lincoln's timing demonstrated a mastery of political communication—remarkable inasmuch as he responded at all, but even more so that he chose to do so via a competing newspaper as well as via a telegraphic transmission. The means and methods used also signaled an open challenge to Greeley, suggesting that readers other than the *Tribune*'s regulars, who in this case would have included abolitionists and radicals, were a more worthy audience for his response. Perhaps most significant of all, Lincoln waited for the right time to demonstrate that he could both preserve the Union and free the slaves, seeing the bloody battle between General George B. McClellan's Army of the Potomac and Confederate general

Robert E. Lee at the Battle of Antietam (or Sharpsburg) in Maryland as the appropriate moment that Seward had wisely recommended. In the fight on September 17, 1862, both sides suffered more than 23,000 combined casualties in the deadliest day—before or since—in American history.[40] Although Union troops died in greater numbers than Lee's, the battle was considered a draw, perhaps at best a tactical victory for McClellan, who forced Lee's men to retreat but then failed to pursue them and deliver a crushing blow. Regardless, Lincoln saw signs that the North could carry on a fight and inflict severe damage to Lee's formidable record of consecutive victories.

Within the week, Lincoln's cabinet met to refine the draft of the edict Lincoln had developed in July, and on September 22, Lincoln issued a preliminary Emancipation Proclamation. On September 23, after having published a call for Lincoln to begin "recognizing, obeying, and enforcing the laws," the *Tribune* celebrated what appeared to be, in Greeley's mind, the president's conversion to the abolitionist cause with extensive coverage of the event.[41] After the fact, Greeley claimed he had understood that the president was deliberating emancipation before Antietam, but publicly, Greeley was recognized as having helped to make abolition a goal of the war. His own editorials proclaimed that the edict would usher in a new era of freedom, a recurring phrase in both the lexicons of Lincoln and the *Tribune*, and that it would lead to the end of the war.[42]

While the Emancipation Proclamation did provide the necessary framework for the eventual end of slavery, the constitutional amendment that did so—as well as the end of the war itself—was still years away. In fact, as quickly as February 1863, Lincoln said to Greeley that he feared the edict had done little to affect the course of the war, adding, however, that it had clearly helped boost the stature of the Union in the eyes of other nations.[43]

For months, battles continued to rage, and simply hoping for an end to the near-constant bloodshed became as much of a struggle as the war itself. After a devastating Union defeat at Fredericksburg, Virginia, in December 1862 and McClellan's repeated failures to smash Robert E. Lee's Army of Northern Virginia, Lincoln's war goals still lay in doubt. By the summer of 1863, Confederate troops under Lee's command had advanced onto northern soil, posing a direct threat to Washington, D.C., and putting the continued existence of the Union itself in jeopardy.

Beginning July 1, 1863, Union forces met Lee's threat outside the town of Gettysburg, Pennsylvania, and accounts of the confrontation began flooding newspapers in the following days. By July 4, the eighty-seventh commemoration of the nation's founding, it was clear that an epic battle had taken place, a three-day event involving more than 160,000 American soldiers. Newspapers around the country filled their pages with reports, maps, drawings, and a steady stream of updates from correspondents and witnesses to the event. From all accounts, Union forces had turned back the rebel invasion, marking a turning point in the war. This, combined with General Ulysses S. Grant's concurrent victory (July 4, 1863) in Vicksburg, Mississippi, which effectively allowed the North to control the Mississippi River and sealed its success in the western theater, allowed Union victories for the duration of the war to become more common than defeats.

Lincoln privately reacted to the news of the Vicksburg victory with satisfied joy, writing that with control of the Mississippi, "The Father of Waters again goes unvexed to the sea."[44] He more publicly promoted the success of the Army of the Potomac at Gettysburg, issuing an official reaction almost immediately that described the victory as a great success and worthy of the highest honor while at the same time offering condolences to loved ones of those who had died.[45] However, in the days that followed—between July 4 and July 14—the president also wrote more than a dozen letters to both high-ranking members of the military and his cabinet that reflected a mixture of regret and disbelief that General Lee's armies had once again managed to escape.

New York's leading newspapers—the *Herald*, *Times*, and *Tribune*—meanwhile provided similar perspectives on the events at Gettysburg, inasmuch as each was generally hopeful and at the same time humbled by tremendous costs to both the combatants and the citizenry. Bennett's *Herald* recognized Gettysburg as a "Great Victory Won!" and one that "settled the fate of the rebellion"; Raymond's *Times* described it as a "splendid triumph" and the Army of the Potomac's "greatest victory."[46] Likewise, Greeley described the battle as the "most terrific fight of the war" and announced "the complete, overwhelming, magnificent victory of the Army of the Potomac."[47] But earlier in the year, Greeley had also already concluded that the war was hopeless and began advocating a restoration of the Union to its previous state. As a result, Greeley's response to Gettysburg, the oddest of them all, was to publish high-handed calls for the president to act decisively alongside columns that suggested the war—despite the victory in Pennsylvania—was still lost, with the *Tribune* essentially arguing less than a year from its celebration of the Emancipation Proclamation that Lincoln should rescind the edict.

Perhaps Greeley was attempting to show some measure of consistency in maintaining a position he had developed before Gettysburg, or perhaps, more likely, the war was taking a toll on his senses—whichever one, he still maintained a level of respect for Lincoln. Indeed, Greeley was not always negative in his assessment of Lincoln, editorializing in 1862, for example, that Lincoln's mind worked extraordinarily well and saw strategy that other politicians and military leaders tended to miss.[48] The president, perhaps alone, Greeley wrote, had recognized that the war might suppress the southern rebellion, but the North could never claim victory as long as slavery continued to exist. He also noted after Gettysburg that Lincoln had spoken in Washington and—also overwhelmed at the events in Pennsylvania—had humbly said, "Gentlemen, this is a glorious theme, and the occasion for speech, but I am not prepared to make one worthy of the occasion."[49]

The process of burying and reburying bodies from the Gettysburg battlefield took months, and in some cases even years—Confederate soldiers who died in the battle would remain scattered in field burials until the early 1870s, when southern organizations began the process of reburial. Many of the bodies were carefully moved from the Pennsylvania site to cemeteries in North and South Carolina and Georgia, and most of the Confederate dead were finally buried at Hollywood Cemetery in Richmond, Virginia, in a special section set aside specifically for the casualties of Gettysburg.[50]

But in November 1863, to commemorate the dedication of the site on which federal troops had died to save the Union from almost

certain defeat, Lincoln went on to deliver a speech that still reso-
nates as among his most famous acts as president. From all accounts,
the president did not know that when he delivered the Gettysburg
Address, a speech to dedicate the national burial ground, it would
become one of the most quoted pieces of oratory in American history;
however, he clearly thought through the importance of every word
he spoke, drafting and revising his speech as a master wordsmith.
He delivered the oration on November 19 in little more than two
minutes with about 270 words, espousing the principles of equality
established at the founding of the nation and defining the struggle
of the Civil War as "a new birth of freedom."[51] He called upon those
in attendance, as well as subsequent generations, to hold a government of the people, by the people, and for the people among their
sacred charges. Lincoln's words, in the century and a half since their
oration, have taken new meanings for those who have interpreted
them, but a recurring theme, which he drew from the Declaration
of Independence, became a timeless reminder of his leadership for
all those who have ruminated upon it: "All men are created equal."

Niagara Failures

While newspapers in the North gave the president's Gettysburg Address mixed reviews, Greeley, increasingly distraught by the war's
incessancy, had already preemptively written William Cornell Jewett,
a Peace Democrat from Maine who had offered to help establish ties
between representatives of the North and South in efforts to negotiate peace.[52] Greeley suggested in the correspondence that he might
appoint himself to act as an official spokesperson and that such talks
must take place between official representatives but that the Confederates must take the initiative without involvement from Great
Britain or France. "I can consider no man a friend of the Union,"
were the letter's concluding words, "who makes a parade of peace
propositions, or peace agitation, prior to such action."[53]

In the spring of 1864, Greeley had described Lincoln in unflattering terms, as unequipped to manage the challenges that faced the
nation.[54] In March, a group of Republican radicals and abolitionists
met in New York to adopt a platform to promote John C. Frémont

in a bid for the presidency. Frémont later withdrew from consideration as a candidate, but only after Greeley had lent support to those who sought to prevent Lincoln from serving another term.[55] Greeley reiterated his opposition to Lincoln when General McClellan initially began receiving support as the Democratic nominee for the presidency. But McClellan quickly became unattractive to members of both parties when the Democrats adopted a platform that advocated peace, even if it called for "Union with Slavery" (a proposition that in the end most voters simply could not accept). Throughout the summer of 1864, Greeley persisted in attempting to set up a convention for an alternative presidential candidate, one who would defeat Lincoln in the election. "Mr. Lincoln is already beaten," Greeley wrote. "He cannot be elected. And we must have another ticket to save us from utter overthrow."[56]

Had General Sherman not conquered Atlanta late in the summer of 1864, Greeley would have most likely seen his prediction fulfilled, as Lincoln's reelection hinged on the stunning, near conclusive blow to the Confederacy. But McClellan's mismanagement of his political campaign—in a strange way reminiscent of his miscalculations as the head of the Army of the Potomac—also helped Lincoln's chances. When it became clear that McClellan's candidacy offered at best a political stalemate (much like the battles he had waged in war) rather than a viable alternative to Lincoln's efforts, Greeley joined those who had flirted with the Democratic opposition. In September, he made an about-face and declared that the *Tribune* would "fly the banner of Abraham Lincoln for the next presidency, choosing that far rather than Disunion and a quarter century of wars."[57]

After months of hectoring from Greeley, Lincoln had apparently had enough when, in an affront to Lincoln's war objectives, Greeley had used the *Tribune* to call on England, France, and even Switzerland to intervene and bring the fighting to an end. Greeley meant right, Lincoln had said to Illinois representative Shelby M. Cullom, but he had made "almost as much trouble as the whole Southern Confederacy."[58] In response, instead of silencing Greeley, Lincoln asked the *Tribune* editor to work with representatives of the Confederate government toward a peace settlement. Although the mission was futile—and

Lincoln knew it would be—the appointment secured the endorsement from the *Tribune* for Lincoln's reelection bid. When newspaper editor and Ohio congressman James Ashley objected to Greeley's mission, Lincoln responded: "Don't worry; nothing will come of it."[59]

The *Tribune* editor was to meet with Confederate emissaries on the Canadian side of Niagara Falls with orders from Lincoln to help arrange discussions with the Confederate president for the end of the war. "If you can find any person anywhere professing to have any proposition of Jefferson Davis in writing, for peace, embracing the restoration of the Union and the abandonment of slavery, whatever else it embraces," Lincoln wrote, "say to him he may come to me with you."[60]

Greeley soon discovered that the Confederates took no such negotiations seriously; after weeks of pursuing what he thought were grounds for a lasting peace, without having received any indication that the Confederate representatives were interested, he wrote in July 1864 again to Jewett, who acted as a quasi-mediator between Greeley and the Confederate representatives. Greeley's new correspondence gave Jewett the impression that Lincoln had empowered him to negotiate as a representative of the Union. Greeley suggested that the sheer economic weight of the war would lead to the ruin of both the North and South, and Lincoln had commissioned him to seek measures to avoid these catastrophic results. He then suggested his own "Plan of Adjustment," a proposal that included a restored Union, the utter abolition of slavery, complete amnesty for all political offenses, and the restoration of citizenship to all. In addition, Greeley proposed a grant of $400 million to the Confederates that would compensate for the losses of slaveholders, plus the restoration of representation for the South in the House.[61]

Upon receiving word of the proposals, both Lincoln and the southern negotiators naturally and thoroughly dismissed them, as Greeley had not even bothered to verify if they had met the approval of either Lincoln or Davis. In fact, upon receiving word of Greeley's exploits, Lincoln wrote two letters on the same day. One indicated his disappointment that not only had no progress been made but also Greeley had, apparently, willfully disregarded instructions. The other stated simply, "I was not expecting you to send me a letter, but to bring me a man or men."[62] The southern representatives had taken Greeley's proposal no less seriously. "It must be confessed that Mr. Greeley, in his hysterical, deluded, and quixotic course in this affair, cuts a shabby and pitiable figure," one wrote. "He also bitterly reproaches Mr. Lincoln for the whole past, and insists upon it that nine tenths of the whole American people, North and South, are sick of slaughter and anxious for peace on almost any terms; that a peace might have been made last month by 'an honest, sincere effort,' but it was now doubtful."[63]

By August 1864, Lincoln had given up on the efforts, writing Greeley that he had received word that Jefferson Davis had no interest in negotiations. Upon the collapse of talks, Greeley sought to exploit his own mistakes by publishing the contents of the letters between Lincoln and himself. He wrote Lincoln, requesting his permission—rather insisting upon it—to print the contents in their entirety. Lincoln first responded that he would not object to publication of the letters but believed that certain details about the meetings would put in danger certain war objectives as well as demoralize readers in the North. "With the suppression of a few passages in your letters in regard to which I think you and I would not disagree," Lincoln wrote, "I should be glad of the publication."[64] Greeley persisted, insisting that he would publish all of the material or none at all, to which Lincoln responded days later, "Herewith is a full copy of the correspondence, and which I have had privately printed, but not made public. The parts of your letters which I wish suppressed are only those which, as I think, give too gloomy an aspect to our cause, and those which present the carrying of elections as a motive of action. I have, as you see, drawn a red pencil over the parts I wish suppressed."[65]

Exasperated—already anticipating Greeley's response—Lincoln turned to Henry Raymond, a stalwart supporter of the administration whom the president had learned he could trust in confidence. "I have proposed to Mr. Greeley that the Niagara correspondence be published, suppressing only the parts of his letter over which the red pencil is drawn in the copy which herewith send," he wrote. "He declines giving his consent to the publication of his letters unless these parts be published with the rest. I have concluded that it is better for *me* to submit, for the time, to the consequences of the false position in which I consider he has placed me, than to subject the *country* to the consequences of publishing these discouraging and injurious parts" (Lincoln's emphasis).[66] Lincoln included in the correspondence a copy of the letters, not intending Raymond to publish them but for reference purposes only.

Newspapers throughout the North eventually did publish the letters, marking what Greeley must have thought was a victory, although he clearly had motives other than protection of press freedoms in mind. Raymond, upon seeing the letters published on front pages of leading newspapers, reportedly exploded with rage over what he perceived as the recklessness of his colleagues in the press. Replying to why he did not condemn the printing of the letters, Lincoln said, "Yes, all the newspapers will publish my letter, and so will Greeley. The next day he will take a line and comment upon it, and he will keep it up, in that way, until, at the end of three weeks, I will be convicted out of my own mouth of all the things which he charges against me. No man, whether he be private citizen or President of the United States, can successfully carry on a controversy with a great newspaper, and escape destruction, unless he owns a newspaper equally great, with a circulation in the same neighborhood."[67]

Indeed, the incident marked a formal souring of Lincoln's attitude toward Greeley. For years, since the *Tribune* had first vacillated in its support of the president, alternating that support with inconsistent criticisms, Lincoln had tolerated Greeley as a valuable ally, despite his eccentricities. However, in an August 19, 1864, cabinet meeting, the president resigned himself to the fact that Greeley had worn out his usefulness. He was like "an old shoe—good for nothing new, whatever he has been," Lincoln said, "so rotten that nothing can be done with him. He is not truthful; the stitches all tear out." He later bitterly complained that Greeley had acted in bad faith not only for attempting to negotiate a settlement on his own terms but also for continuing to attack the administration's prosecution of the war.[68]

In fact, Greeley's attempt at peacemaking was so heavy-handed that Secretary Seward threatened to prosecute him under the Logan Act, which prohibited American citizens from negotiating with foreign representatives. However, Lincoln discouraged the action, joking that Greeley did more to aid in the successful prosecution of the war than he could have done in any other way, as the South, prior to this time, had engaged successfully in a defensive war, but Greeley's over-earnest peace efforts had enticed them to go on the offense, resulting in the Confederacy's defeat.[69]

In a final insult to Greeley's efforts, he again took criticism from his rivals at the *Chicago Tribune*, which published details from Greeley's travels to Canada that suggested he had quaked in terror in his writing to Lincoln. The accounts noted that Greeley's own writings at the time had focused on the "bleeding, bankrupt, almost dying" Union that longed for peace and shuddered "at the prospect of fresh conscriptions, of further wholesale devastation, and of new rivers of human blood." The language in both Greeley's letters and those from Lincoln indicated in the estimation of the Chicago editors that Greeley's fear of the Confederate negotiators was matched only by Lincoln's contempt for Greeley. Lincoln must have arranged the entire mission, the editorial concluded, simply to let Greeley realize that his vacillating and inconsistent calls for both a prosecution of the war and an end to it were "his own folly."[70]

As the war came to a brutal close in the final months of 1864 and early 1865, the consistent all-news format of the *New York Times* trumped in the minds of many readers Greeley's less predictable (and sometimes wrongheaded) sentiments. Henry Raymond had aggressively coordinated Lincoln's reelection drive by heading efforts to raise money from Republican supporters. The efforts earned him the position of chair of the Republican National Committee, and from 1865 to 1867, he served as a member of the U.S. House. The *Herald*, meanwhile, remained New York's leading newspaper, and although James Gordon Bennett had supported in 1864 the Democratic candidate George McClellan, Lincoln respected the professionalism of the newspaper's war coverage. In February 1865, Lincoln offered Bennett a ministerial appointment to France, which Bennett declined, writing Lincoln that he appreciated the offer but doubted that, at his age, he could perform the duties required, preferring to maintain his newspaper instead.

Lincoln had grown transcendentally fatalistic about the nation's experience, as well as about his own personal tragedies during the war—in 1862, his eleven-year-old son Willie died and his wife Mary's mental health subsequently declined. Such resignation to the condition of humanity could account for his ability to forgive Greeley's lapses of judgment. In March 1865, the two men met for a final time, but the president apparently did not make known to Greeley his plans to appoint him to the position of postmaster general, a position long desired by the long-suffering would-be politician. The most significant item to come from the meeting was, perhaps, one of Greeley's most poignant observations of the president—specifically, his description of Lincoln's countenance. Lincoln's face was "haggard with care, and seemed with thought and trouble," Greeley wrote. "It looked care-plowed, tempest-tossed, and weather-beaten, as if he were some tough old mariner." Greeley feared the stress of the war had become so burdensome on the president's health that Lincoln—just two weeks before his eventual assassination—simply could not survive it.[71]

CONCLUSION: RE-REMEMBERING
LINCOLN AND GREELEY

A s the war entered its final months and only time separated the
Union from victory, Abraham Lincoln managed to shed at
least some of the excruciating strain that Horace Greeley had sensed
in their final meeting. Lincoln's reelection in November 1864, combined with Union general William Tecumseh Sherman's devastating
campaign through Georgia and the Carolinas, had put the end of
the war in sight. Discussions in the North and in Congress turned to
life after the war and—with glimmers not felt for years—to hope of
what might become of the restored nation. With the major cities of
Virginia reconquered by Union forces and General Ulysses S. Grant's
successes in both the eastern and western theaters of the war, General Robert E. Lee surrendered the Confederate Army of Northern
Virginia on April 9, 1865. As news that the war had ended reached
readers in the North, Greeley's *Tribune* reported that the streets of
New York City were filled with cheers lasting the entire night.[1]

In the months following the November 1864 election, Lincoln's
harshest critics, which had at times included Greeley, recognized
that the president had at least begun to secure a Union victory and
shifted from attacks to more general support of the administration.
James Gordon Bennett, for his part, remained focused primarily on
reporting war news, telling readers of the *New York Herald* that they
could vote for their own candidate instead of following what would
have ordinarily been his endorsement of the Democratic candidate.

Bennett was doubtless gratified that Lincoln had offered him the position of minister to France, the most prestigious post Lincoln had offered to any of the New York editors.

Greeley, who waited in vain for an appointment to Lincoln's cabinet after having been told he had reason to expect one, had learned to live with the disappointment of exclusion from Lincoln's closest advisors. Lincoln had correctly reasoned that Greeley and Seward simply could not work together and that, as long as Seward remained his secretary of state, Greeley—whether or not he knew why—simply could play no direct role in the administration.

Lincoln's Martyrdom

Despite the perception of Greeley, much of which was mixed, with his faithful readers remaining loyal admirers and his critics having pegged him as a self-serving office seeker, Ward Hill Lamon, a longtime friend of Lincoln's, observed that the *Tribune* editor "had power" over the president.[2] Lamon, as a self-appointed bodyguard of the president, had made it his job to pay close attention to those who surrounded Lincoln, but on the night of April 14, 1865, Lincoln had sent him on an assignment to Richmond, Virginia.

Before a night at the theater with his wife, the president—for the first time in years—took the opportunity to relax during a carriage ride. He spoke of early days in a log cabin, of his old Springfield home, and of his days working in a law office, Mary Lincoln recalled. "The tension under which he had for so long been kept was removed," she said, "and he was like a boy out of school."[3] Later that Good Friday night, the couple attended the play *Our American Cousin* at Ford's Theatre in Washington, where an assassin fired a bullet into the president's head and killed him. The nation grieved with a sorrow as profound as that which had become so familiar to families who had lost loved ones during the war.

Greeley was naturally devastated, with the eulogies to Lincoln revealing an uncommon perspective, with little of the shock, disbelief, and horror communicated nationally. Greeley, instead, reacted with words of respect and emotion. "He filled a larger space in the public eye than any American before him, partly because of the stupendous events in which he bore a conspicuous part," he wrote, suggesting few graves would be more visited "or bedewed with the tears of a people's prouder, fonder affection."[4] Lincoln, in Greeley's most astute observation, was a man and not a superman—an assessment that students of history almost 150 years later can trust in many ways more than the president's most worshipful contemporaries.

The *New York Tribune*'s first announcement of Lincoln's assassination came in columns separated by black bands, which, beginning April 15, continued for thirty days with updates on the president's death and the national mourning that followed it. Unlike the bulk of content published in newspapers throughout the nation, Greeley interpreted Lincoln's life not only in terms of his presidency but also in terms of what preceded it. Among his most widely read reflections on Lincoln published in the *Tribune*, "The Nation's Loss" (April 17), "Mr. Lincoln's Fame" (April 19), "The People's Lament" (April 21), and "What He Did Not Say" (April 24) revealed the editor's sincere interest in preserving Lincoln's humanity. Greeley, in his own words, had hoped "to make the real Lincoln, with his thoroughly human good and ill, his virtues and his imperfections, more instructive and more helpful to ordinary humanity than his unnatural, celestial, apotheosized shadow ever was or could be."[5]

It should be remembered that prior to Lincoln's death, other newspapers in the North, in the South, and in Europe as well had cast aspersions not only on his politics and his war policy but also on his character, most much more harsh than anything ever published in the *Tribune*. Yet, the ensuing amount of newspaper content devoted to Lincoln's assassination was unprecedented. "Today every loyal heart must suffer the terrible shock, and swell with overburdening grief at the calamity which has been permitted to befall us in the assassination of the Chief Magistrate," read the *New York World*—after the same newspaper had (wrongly) blasted Lincoln less than a year before for allegedly joking about the bloodshed at Antietam. With the close of the war, and in light of Lincoln's uncommon ability to seek no retribution against his enemies, the *World* reversed its tone, describing his death as if the nation's first soldier had fallen by a hostile bullet.[6]

The events reverberated internationally as well, with editors in Europe offering virtually unanimous sympathy. In London, the *Morning Star* expressed regret that the British had not appreciated Lincoln's role as a leader until he had died, confessing shame over the fact that their writers had degraded him during the war and criticized him as a simple "foreign patriot." Likewise, the *London Daily News*, which had previously described Lincoln as an "imbecile," realized that his character ought to inspire reverence. In France, the *Époque* described the president as a martyr who had paid for the Union victory with his blood.[7]

With Lincoln's body at the White House on Easter Sunday, 1865, the *New York Herald* soberly recognized that the press had played a role in the assassination—one that went beyond simply reporting it. It was "clear as day" that the origin of Lincoln's murder could be found in the "fiendish and malignant spirit developed and fostered by the rebel press North and South," James Gordon Bennett editorialized. "That press has, in the most devilish manner, urged men to the commission of this very deed."[8] Lincoln's body left Washington, D.C., on a train draped in black. Stopping at cities en route to Springfield, Illinois, the procession was met by countless mourners paying their final respects. Lincoln's burial party finally laid his body to rest at Oak Ridge Cemetery on May 4, 1865.

Reconstructing Reconstruction

Vice President Andrew Johnson assumed the presidency upon Lincoln's death and was charged with the task of rebuilding the nation according to plans laid by his predecessor; however, unlike Lincoln, Johnson, a Tennessee Democrat, consistently sided with the interests of white southerners, infuriating Republicans in Congress who sought to enforce Reconstruction measures. But Johnson did share at least one trait with Lincoln: both had passed (for different reasons and under different circumstances) on the opportunity to appoint Greeley to their cabinets. "I always considered [Greeley] a good enough editor before the war, although I never agreed with him; but in all other matters he seemed to me like a whale ashore," Johnson said. "He runs to goodness of heart so much as to produce infirmity of mind."[9] While Greeley at first had sided with Johnson and opposed the Radical Republicans, by the end of 1866 he began publishing regular condemnations of the administration, which was, in the *Tribune*'s words, the weakest of all preceding presidencies.

Greeley had meanwhile begun a history of the Civil War titled *The American Conflict*, which he eventually published in two volumes. He had released the first part, covering the years leading to war, in 1864, and reviews of it generally described it as an accurate compilation of documents he had accumulated in his capacity as an editor, an amateur historian, and a witness to events. However, the second volume, published in 1866, found a less receptive audience. The national sense of bitterness over the loss of Lincoln had not yet subsided, and Greeley's critics had become aware of the rumored tensions between him and the late president, including the disclosure of his frenzied letter after Bull Run, the fiascoes surrounding his peace negotiations in Canada, and the alleged fallout over Greeley's exclusion from the cabinet. Greeley had promoted *The American Conflict* through the *Tribune*'s various resources, inserting advertisements for it as a history he hoped would be "entirely right on every point."[10] But the *Chicago Tribune*, among the most vocal critics, was correct in noting that Greeley had failed in at least one obvious respect: he had paid scant attention to the role of Lincoln, who was, of course, the primary figure in the war. The newspaper noted that Greeley's history consisted primarily of news stories from Greeley's own editorial perspective, "full of the imperfect information which necessarily characterizes a report for a daily paper when it deals with questions which go to make history."[11]

To a certain extent, Greeley contributed directly to the public perception that he indeed harbored bitter feelings about a lifetime of exclusion from major political activities; however, in other respects, he maintained Lincoln's memory more faithfully than did the president's most vocal supporters. In the same year he published the second volume of his Civil War history, Greeley again (in no likely coincidence) sought a seat in the Senate, promoting himself in the winter of 1866–67 by advocating "universal amnesty" for former Confederate leaders. And even though Lincoln had clearly said he intended to restore the Union "with malice toward none" and "charity toward all," Greeley's positions hurt him, as the most common position among his fellow Republicans was to hold the South in check with a new generation of reconstructed state and local governments that disavowed sympathies for the former Confederacy. At the same time, in also supporting the right for African Americans to vote, Greeley lost the support of New York's Democrats, and adding to a lifetime of election defeats—punctuated only by his short term in the Thirtieth Congress with Lincoln—Greeley lost his bid. In typical fashion, he had received some of the harshest criticism of his campaign from the Lincoln loyalists at the *Chicago Tribune*, who wrote, "For twenty-five years he has been a marplot in council; an unreliable commander in action; a misanthrope in victory, and a riotous disorganizer in defeat."[12]

Upon losing his second bid for the Senate, Greeley continued to promote amnesty for the South, including for former Confederate president Jefferson Davis. In 1867, Greeley acted upon his stated positions by signing Davis's bail bond and, in doing so, lost thousands of *Tribune* readers.[13] In an attempt to restore his increasingly battered image, Greeley published in 1868 the autobiography *Recollections of a Busy Life*, addressing, along with his lifetime of achievements, old allegations that had resurfaced since Lincoln's assassination—namely, that he had supported Lincoln's nomination simply out of spite for Seward, his former partner. Greeley's story, as he told it, did contain an impressive collection of historical observations, not only about his own life but also about the events that had surrounded him. Of special interest to Lincoln's supporters—as well as to historians of subsequent generations—Greeley minimized his efforts at the Chicago convention, attributing Lincoln's victory primarily to his supporters in Illinois: "I did much less than was popularly supposed."[14]

In 1868, Greeley also penned a tribute to Lincoln, one of the few first-person accounts from either of the two men about their relationship in politics and the press.[15] Upon its posthumous publication in the *Century*, readers recognized that Greeley's final testament to Lincoln included indications that he had come to terms with his exclusion from the president's cabinet. Although the slight had clearly bothered him during the Civil War, he recognized that Lincoln's decisions were sound.[16] In Greeley's estimate, Lincoln was "simply a plain, true, earnest, patriotic man, gifted with eminent common sense, which, in its wide range, gave a hand to shrewdness on the one hand, humor on the other, and which allied him intimately, warmly, with the masses of mankind."[17]

The Final Campaign

Although the physical battles of the Civil War had ceased years before the 1868 election of General Ulysses S. Grant to the presidency, many of the most intense issues addressed by the press in the years leading up to the war continued to influence the course of the nation. From a northern perspective, editors sought to legitimize the battles in which thousands of Yankee soldiers had died, and from a southern one, editors in major cities saw the efforts of the federal government, as exercised under the administration of the former Union general, as a continuation of the impositions by Washington before the war.[18]

Greeley had supported Grant during his first term, an administration most notably marked by Grant's attempts to enforce the Reconstruction Amendments that guaranteed emancipation, equal protection, and suffrage rights for former slaves. But by 1871, Greeley and members of the liberal wing of the Republican Party had come to resent what they considered Grant's subservience to hard-line Republicans who wanted to punish the South. The group cited among its complaints the president's indifference to civil service reform and the corruption of his administration. Opposing primarily Grant's military-based Reconstruction efforts and his expansionist foreign policy, the *Tribune*, along with Senators Carl Schurz of Missouri, Lyman Trumbull of Illinois, and Charles Sumner of Massachusetts, began encouraging in the later part of the president's first term a dissident movement of Republicans.[19]

In May 1872, the group formed the Liberal Republican Party and, at their convention in Cincinnati, Ohio, picked Greeley as the party's presidential nominee, calling for the restoration of the nation more closely in line, they believed, with the ideals that Lincoln had advocated. This collection of northeastern Republicans, originally only a faction, gained momentum when mainstream newspapers began entertaining Greeley's chances in the fall election. "The only Republican who has made, or is likely to make any overtures to the rebel and Democratic element, is Greeley," the *Chicago Tribune* observed. "[W]e look upon Mr. Greeley's nomination by the Democratic Party, if they adopt the Ohio platform, as not beyond the domain of probable things."[20] When the weakened Democratic Party met to select its nominee in Baltimore on July 10, 1872, seeking a viable candidate to represent southern interests (considering his previous attempts to promote amnesty for Confederates), Greeley did indeed emerge as its pick, marking the only time in U.S. history when a major party adopted through a separate endorsement a third party candidate. In another twist in an already unusual series of events, the *Chicago Tribune* also endorsed Greeley, but only after first dismissing his candidacy as a fluke.[21]

Greeley, who formerly had supported the Whig and Republican Parties and had consistently opposed the Democrats, had won endorsements from two parties to which he had previously declared no loyalty. Yet his acceptance speech at the Liberal Republican convention reflected his faith in the possibility of rebuilding the nation in the interests of all Americans, North and South, and of guaranteeing the political rights of all. The people were determined to have a truly national reconstruction, a "New Departure" from jealousy, strife, and hatred, he said, and "in the joyful consciousness that they are and must henceforth remain brethren," he resigned his *Tribune* editorship to begin what would prove to be his final campaign.[22]

Greeley's bid for the presidency began hopefully enough, promoting "Universal Amnesty," which made it possible for southern Democrats to support him because he promised to restore rights to former Confederate officers; however, voters in the South were at the same time alienated by the call, as it entailed the enforcement of rights for freed slaves. In the North, Greeley's competitors in the newspaper industry exploited his candidacy as an opportunity to build their own circulations with sensational attacks on his character. His critics had little trouble finding controversial editorials published in the *Tribune* during the previous forty years, pointing to them (in many cases out of context) as indicative of Greeley's radicalism.

By the end of the summer of 1872, the press campaign against Greeley degenerated into a mudslinging melee, epitomized by the anti-Greeley cartoons of Thomas Nast in *Harper's Weekly*. Greeley did have support from the anti-Grant cartoons of Matt Morgan in *Frank Leslie's Illustrated Newspaper*, which branded Grant a dictator and a drunk, and of course from his own *Tribune*, but more powerful were condemnations from Grant's supporters that depicted Greeley as a traitor and a fool.[23] The incessant assaults on his character took such a mental and physical toll on him that toward the end of his campaign, he complained, "I have been assailed so bitterly that I hardly knew whether I was running for the presidency or the penitentiary."[24]

Still a candidate, Greeley attempted to return to work at his *Tribune* office during the final weeks of the campaign, but managing editor Whitelaw Reid, who worried about Greeley's deteriorating health and the negative effect it might have on the newspaper's circulation, forced him to relinquish the post. In October, Greeley's health indeed worsened after his wife, Mary, died. Compounded with the election returns—Grant won in a landslide, leaving Greeley with just six of thirty-seven states and 44 percent of the popular vote—Greeley fell mortally ill, suffering the stress of an exhausting campaign, the loss of his wife, and the devastating election results. He was interned in an asylum in Pleasantville, New York, as his condition deteriorated into a severe physical and mental breakdown. In one account of his final days, he spoke with Reid and cried, "You son of a bitch, you stole my newspaper." But according to Reid, Greeley said in his final words, "I know my redeemer liveth."[25] Hopeless and ill, Horace Greeley died November 29, 1872.

Lincoln and Greeley Memorialized

For James Parton, who had reissued his Greeley biography in time for the 1872 election, the best way to summarize the *Tribune* editor's life had been in his influence on workers, the print industry, and the entire nation. "He began life as a workingman. As a workingman, he found out, and he experienced the disadvantages of the workingman's condition. He rose from the ranks to a position of commanding influence," Parton wrote. "But he ceased to be a workingman *with* workingmen, only to become a workingman *for* workingmen" (Parton's emphasis).[26]

At his December 4 funeral, critics who had made sport out of Greeley and admirers alike mourned the loss of a humanitarian spirit and the nation's best-known editor. A large gathering of common people and local, state, and national leaders, including President Grant and Chief Justice Salmon Chase, attended the event.[27] Abolitionist Henry Ward Beecher, brother of *Uncle Tom's Cabin* author Harriet Beecher Stowe, eulogized Greeley as "a man who died of a broken heart," while the *Tribune* paid tribute to Greeley with special editions and memorial biographies.

Greeley's death brought together former political rivals who began to reevaluate not only Greeley's life but the lives of those he had touched as well. With Reconstruction emerging as a disillusioning experience for those who had hoped to restore the Union according to Lincoln's plans, the memory of the deceased president was also invoked in eulogies to his late friend in the press. Among the torrents of praise published in honor of Greeley, Democrats and Republicans (the Liberal Republican Party had died with Greeley), as well as northerners and southerners, found a way to look beyond the idiosyncrasies of the *Tribune* publisher and rank him among Lincoln's peers. One such eulogy, from Theodore H. Cuyler, a Presbyterian minister from Brooklyn, put Lincoln and Greeley together as relatives in more than merely a figurative manner. "Since the death of good 'Uncle Abe,' no death in America has produced such a deep and general feeling as the death of that extraordinary man whom many of us used affectionately to call 'Uncle Horace,'" Cuyler said. "No two men understood the 'common people' as well as they did, or could reach the average capacity so exactly by pen and tongue." Cuyler also connected their stories in the tragic ways that both men died: "The brain of the one was pierced by a pistol-ball, the brain of the other was pierced by an acute and deadly grief that killed as surely as any bullet ever fired," he said. "Both were followed to their graves by vast multitudes of sorrowing mourners."[28]

By the early twentieth century, both men had even become heroes to some in the South, where previous generations had considered them enemies of the Confederacy. The dedication of a memorial statue on February 3, 1914, at Chappaqua, New York, where Greeley had farmed from 1854 to 1872, included a speech delivered by southern-born William G. McAdoo, treasury secretary for Woodrow Wilson. At a time when the rise of nationalism in Europe had escalated to the brink of war, McAdoo classed Lincoln and Greeley as American heroes of equal status. "No two men on the northern side of the great conflict between the states hold a higher place in the esteem and admiration of the South than Lincoln and Greeley," McAdoo said. "Wholly unlike in temperament, they were amazingly alike in their love for the common people, their detestation of wrong in all of its phases, their unselfish devotion to the public weal, their lofty and inspired patriotism." McAdoo recognized Greeley's weaknesses, his "vanities arising from a craving for political power which led him into many errors," but just as Greeley had astutely noted in his memoirs of Lincoln, McAdoo, in turn, recognized that both the beloved president and the beloved editor were not of another world: "They were not demagogues, but men."[29]

McAdoo's assessment was both fair and accurate inasmuch as both Lincoln and Greeley had considered themselves, in genuine humility, to be lesser men than their shared hero, Henry Clay. Lincoln, who had described himself as "always a [W]hig in politics, and generally on the electoral tickets," had long considered Clay to be his "beau ideal of a statesman, the man for whom I fought all my humble life."[30] Likewise, even after Lincoln's death, Greeley recognized no one as influential on his life or on the course of the United States as "the Great Compromiser," writing simply but powerfully, "I have admired and trusted many statesmen. I profoundly loved Henry Clay."[31]

The virtues and, in more ways, the faults of the mere men described by McAdoo were greatly redefined in the United States, Europe, and elsewhere by the cataclysmic events of World War I. As Americans had been called upon to fight and die for freedom—this time, across the Atlantic—Lincoln's name was invoked to legitimize their sacrifice. While Greeley's contributions could not at the time provide Americans the needed assurance of a trusted leader—one who had grown even stronger in their memory of him—Lincoln's legacy grew in scholarly, political, and popular circles, as readers reexamined his words for clues on how again to make meaning from war.

This shared cultural and historical understanding of the nation's past was made manifest May 30, 1922, at the dedication of the Lincoln Memorial in Washington, D.C. President Warren G. Harding's speech commemorating the event repeated a sentiment from past eulogies that now resonated in stark contrast with the edifice behind him. "There are neither supermen nor demigods in the government of kingdoms, empires, or republics," Harding said. "Abraham Lincoln was no superman." Yet, the twenty-ninth president noted, Lincoln also demonstrated characteristics that placed him in a class not only with the best of his contemporaries but above his most intense critics. "No leader was ever more unsparingly criticized or more bitterly assailed," Harding said of Lincoln. "He was lashed by angry tongues and ridiculed in the press and speech until he drank from as bitter a cup as was ever put to human lips, but his faith was unshaken and his patience never exhausted."[32] Harding made no direct mention of Greeley in his speech, but the senior members of his audience that day, which included hundreds of Union and Confederate veterans now acculturated in a mass media that had summoned Americans to fight in Europe, would have remembered a voice, the *Tribune*, that had also called for peace.

A debate over whether Lincoln or Greeley (or both) overestimated the indebtedness of the nation to Clay belongs perhaps in the classroom or in another book, but what both men clearly did was to live out their separate understandings of what it meant to be a self-made man. While Clay had promoted the idea in his model of the American System, he failed repeatedly in his own quests for the presidency.[33] Lincoln, however, succeeded, as no president before or since, in maintaining a nation on the verge of ruin. And while Clay celebrated the ability of the individual to prosper in the United States, a nation for which he spoke tirelessly to preserve, Greeley worked just as tirelessly—and effectively—to ensure that every individual American had the opportunity to express his or her voice in his *Tribune*, the era's most potent mass media representative. Among those involved in promoting freedom during the war, Greeley was certainly one of the most active and, working under Lincoln's leadership, helped to preserve the Union. But more important, in doing so, the two men also provided for future generations astonishing examples of citizens—not superheroes or demigods—with individual legacies every bit as large as their sum.

NOTES ON SOURCES
NOTES
SELECTED BIBLIOGRAPHY
INDEX

Most biographical accounts since the deaths of both Abraham Lincoln and Horace Greeley have studied the two men by focusing on the life of one and paying only secondary attention to the role of the other. Even though individual biographies of the two have appeared on a regular basis, few (if any) have attempted to interpret the life of each on equal footing, with both contributing in commensurate amounts to a shared legacy rather than merely each to his own. Although compiling a narrative about the lives of both men by simply weaving individual anecdotes from various biographies together may seem tempting, such a method cannot work effectively. Attention to the context in which each source was written, as well as to what each source says about both Lincoln and Greeley, played a role in determining whether or not to include it in this work.

Of the biographies by their contemporaries, the books *Herndon's Lincoln*, written by Lincoln's law partner William Herndon and first published in 1889, and James Parton's *The Life of Horace Greeley*, first published in 1855 and updated in 1872 with information on Greeley's presidential bid, were among the first to which I turned for biographical details.[1] Among the few sources to focus exclusively on their direct relationship is Harlan Hoyt Horner's *Lincoln and Greeley*, and although the book traces a compelling, parallel course in the writings, sayings, and careers of both men, it is also more than fifty years old and lacks a thesis beyond simple comparisons of their ideas. While it is common (and reasonable) to believe that there is "nothing new under the sun," so to speak, in history, sources such as these with both their strengths and the room they left for redevelopment—made *Abraham Lincoln and Horace Greeley* possible.

In reviewing the vast literature on both Lincoln and his contemporaries, Lincoln's legacy, more so than Greeley's, has enjoyed near constant interest both from scholars and in popular circles, but understanding the circumstances in which generations of historians wrote their interpretations helped me determine the role individual sources would play in this work. For example, in 2009 and the years leading up to it, in remembrance of the 200th anniversary of Lincoln's birth, historians published an extraordinary number of works—most respectful, some revisionist, and a few critical. Michael Knox Beran's *Forge of Empires*, a sample of this surge in scholarship, provides a reinterpretation of Lincoln on an international level, juxtaposing his role with those of nationalist leaders in Germany and Russia. "Lincoln called his revolution a 'new birth of freedom.' Bismarck spoke of a revolution accomplished through an expenditure of 'blood and iron.' Alexander implemented what he described as a revolution 'from above,'" Beran writes. "Their revolutions were made in the name of freedom, and were to varying extents consecrated to the freer movement of people, goods, and ideas."[2] Beran's angle is compelling in a contemporary sense (and one worth considering in writing a biography of any nineteenth-century figure) because it puts Lincoln into a global context—one in which he rightfully belongs but one that, until recently, has been paid scant attention.

Of other recent works on Lincoln, many historians cite Michael Burlingame's *Abraham Lincoln: A Life*, a two-volume set of more than 2,000 pages that took over ten years of research and writing, as the most fully documented biography of the man ever written. Burlingame scoured thousands of nineteenth-century newspapers; read hundreds of oral histories, unpublished letters, and journals from Lincoln's contemporaries; and reexamined vast manuscript collections around the country long neglected by the most assiduous of his colleagues. While references to both the *New York Tribune* and Horace Greeley make recurring appearances throughout Burlingame's narrative, his use of an unprecedented number of sources—certainly not press-related alone—makes his work remarkable, providing a sense of the totality of material on Lincoln's life and, in doing so, a clearer understanding of how he influenced history.

More generally, Lincoln biographers have sought to provide peculiar angles for reinterpreting his personal traits. For example, Fred Kaplan, an English professor and biographer of authors, examines Lincoln's literary skills in *Lincoln: The Biography of a Writer*. Kaplan declares Lincoln to be one of the great writers of his day, on a par with Greeley's skills as a publisher, and second perhaps only to Thomas Jefferson as a writing president. Noting that Lincoln was an extraordinary president—inasmuch as we can be relatively certain that he wrote the material attributed to him, unlike a number of other presidents who had paid speechwriters—Kaplan cites an autobiography that Lincoln wrote for the 1860 campaign. Lincoln first submitted the piece to John Locke Scripps, an editor at the *Chicago Tribune*, who revised it, published it, and allowed Greeley to republish it in the *New York Tribune*.[3]

Lincoln maintained active ties to editors, and although the foremost among them was indeed Greeley, he demonstrated a mastery of mass communication in general. Having used the press to his advantage, as well as having demonstrated an understanding of how to address criticisms from it, Lincoln's place in press history has been studied by scholars in a number of disciplines. Among the more widely cited books regarding the role of the press in Lincoln's administration, Robert S. Harper's *Lincoln and the Press* looks at newspapers that supported the war and at those that opposed it; however, like Horner's *Lincoln and Greeley*, it is more than a half-century old and does not focus on a specific set of ideas.

As Lincoln's intellectual match and, more often, his critic in the press, Greeley's legacy has also received renewed interest of late. Ordinarily, biographies of Greeley—such as Glyndon G. Van Deusen's remarkable *Horace Greeley: Nineteenth-Century Crusader*, a treatment of the editor in Van Deusen's series on other leading Whigs—generally present Lincoln and the Civil War as a backdrop for the *Tribune*'s editorial agenda. Among the recent works to recognize the editor, Robert C. Williams's *Horace Greeley: Champion of American Freedom*, similar to Beran's treatment of Lincoln, puts Greeley's career into an international context, devoting attention to Greeley's role in advocating revolutionary movements at home and abroad.[4] Even though counterrevolutions in Europe appeared to have crushed movements for social change during the late 1840s, as Williams notes, many of the reform efforts that Greeley continued to advocate in his *Tribune*, including the distribution of land in the West among the public, came to fruition in following decades.

Greeley's publishing agenda, it has even been argued, set the tone for twenty-first-century news content. As Adam Tuchinsky describes in *Horace Greeley's* New-York Tribune*: Civil War–Era Socialism and the Crisis of Free Labor*—borrowing at least in part from the work of John R. Commons—the *Tribune* featured content now more commonly recognized as "citizen journalism," or as Commons had put it, "constructive democracy."[5] Today, online contributors who write from a range of political persuasions hold—perhaps unknowingly—Greeley's belief in using the press to advance freedom.

Honest students of history will discover that although both men generally tower over their peers—with Lincoln earning a spot as one of the all-time great presidents and Greeley still considered, in *Harper's Weekly's* words, as "the most perfect Yankee the country has ever produced"—their contemporaries did not always hold them in such high regard.[6] Lincoln, it will be remembered, was not even on the ballot in southern states in the 1860 election (in which he won only 40 percent of the national vote). Moreover, he was blasted for the Emancipation Proclamation in both the North and the South and seemed in danger of not winning reelection in 1864. Even Greeley's most faithful readers, at the time, likewise had no defense for his radical views, and his critics thought him a fool—the *New York Herald's* James Gordon Bennett, foremost among them, once described Greeley as the most "unmitigated blockhead connected with the newspaper press."[7]

The path of Lincoln's legacy, more dramatically than Greeley's, has taken various turns over the past 150 years, with not every historian remembering him at the near-deified levels of today. Although he was able to finish only two of the volumes in his ambitious work, Albert J. Beveridge's biography *Abraham Lincoln, 1809–1858* remains a classic example, as well as one of the more controversial treatments of Lincoln's life. Beveridge, unlike many of those who preceded or followed him, expressed in his understanding of Lincoln's politics a sympathy for southern independence by suggesting it was the radicals in the North, not secessionists, who had killed compromise. In Beveridge's estimation, it was the abolitionists, and not the southern fire-eaters as traditionally portrayed, who destroyed the compromise efforts of men such as Henry Clay and Daniel Webster. Moreover, the North allowed movements such as Know-Nothingism and prohibition to flourish, all the while exacerbating relations with the South by making demands for costly internal improvements at the expense of those who did not always directly benefit from them. In Beveridge's account, Stephen A. Douglas, Lincoln's nemesis in other histories, emerged as a hero, with the Little Giant among those who tried desperately to save the Union. At the same time, Beveridge did see greatness in Lincoln, citing his Springfield speech in October 1854, which attacked the Kansas-Nebraska legislation, as displaying "exalted yet restrained eloquence" and the "generosity of spirit which is to be fully realized in the Second Inaugural."[8]

In a similarly revisionist approach to Lincoln's story, James G. Randall and Richard N. Current's monumental four-volume biography *Lincoln the President* established the standard for interpreting previous scholarship, depicting Lincoln's greatest successes as fending off the designs of Radical Republicans, who sought both to destroy the South and to punish it after the war. Randall and Current's version of history pits a conservative Lincoln against adversaries in his own party who posed an even greater threat to his ability to lead than did anyone in the Democratic Party.[9] Among Lincoln's most difficult legal decisions—perhaps still the most controversial exercise of his powers as president—was his suspension of the writ of habeas corpus, which, Randall and Current note, concerned even Lincoln as a potentially dictatorial move and one that members of the press rightfully criticized.[10]

While subsequent generations of students of history have come to know Lincoln as the Great Emancipator, concerns about his management of civil liberties, noted not only by Randall and Current, are still valid, as he remains the only president to have suspended the writ of habeas corpus and to have actively prosecuted and censored opponents in the press.[11] While a number of First Amendment scholars have studied the effect of Lincoln's wartime measures on the press, Mark E. Neely's *The Fate of Liberty: Abraham Lincoln and Civil Liberties*, a 1992 Pulitzer Prize winner, explores masterfully the controversy over Lincoln's relationship with the Constitution. Neely's sympathetic perspective on Lincoln depicts his actions as well-intentioned attempts to address unprecedented wartime issues, including the threat to the nation's capital posed by secessionists in Maryland, the disintegration of public order in the border states, corruption among military contractors, the occupation of hostile Confederate territory, and the outcry against the first draft in U.S. history.[12]

While Neely describes Lincoln as a generally wise ruler, other historians have provided a different perspective on the president, his contemporaries, and the nineteenth century in general by focusing on events beyond human control that surrounded daily lives. Setting a standard for modern biographies, David Herbert Donald's *Lincoln* recognizes the importance of Lincoln's statement to Kentucky editor A. G. Hodges: "I claim not to have controlled events, but confess plainly that events have controlled me."[13] Along this track, Joshua Wolf Shenk's *Lincoln's Melancholy*, another example of a recent examination of events beyond Lincoln's control, provides a compelling medical interpretation of Lincoln's personality, attributing his personal traits to what psychiatrists might recognize as a depressive disorder.[14]

Greeley also was known to suffer from fits of despair, even madness, which contemporaries—and even Greeley himself—described as "brain fever."[15] Williams's *Horace Greeley: Champion of American Freedom* claims, controversially, that Greeley's quirks were attributable to a neurological disorder known as Asperger's syndrome.[16] But whatever the clinical nature of Greeley's ailments, by the midnineteenth century, as press historian James M. Perry notes in his account of Civil War journalists, *A Bohemian Brigade*, "America was chockablock with eccentrics, and Greeley stood head and shoulders above them all."[17]

In studying Lincoln and Greeley—or any other historical personality or issue, for that matter—the researcher also needs to consider, as do readers, certain basic falsehoods that have passed, for one reason or another, into popular memory as something resembling fact. Popular legends, for example, cast Lincoln as a country bumpkin or a virtual failure at everything until he rose to heroic status under difficult circumstances as president. Although these folk versions of his life have attracted admirers of his legacy, an accurate study of his life before 1860 (and of his careers as both an elected official and a lawyer) exposes such legends as misleading, if not entirely false. The popular *Chicken Soup for the Soul*, for example, has helped perpetuate the myth that Lincoln essentially failed at everything before becoming president; however, as generations of historians have demonstrated, the claim is false.[18]

Likewise, myth still tends to riddle Greeley's legacy, as, in many cases, he is still remembered for something that most historians agree he did not even write. The quote most often attributed to the *Tribune* editor, "Go West, young man, go West," in fact was written by Indiana editor John Soule, who, in an 1851 bet, suggested that just about anything in print at the time would be recognized as having come from Greeley's own hand. When the *Tribune* gave wide exposure to Soule's counsel, Greeley did indeed become (and remains to this day) associated with the slogan in popular memory. (Greeley biographer James Parton noted that a line in a column titled "To Aspiring Young Men" only resembled the oft-quoted saying: "If you have no family or friends to aid you, and no prospect opened to you there, turn your face to the Great West, and there build up a home and fortune.")[19]

Despite a number of accounts that have attempted to cast them as anything other than friends, Lincoln and Greeley were political and intellectual allies, and this fact deserves a final note on the sources used for this monograph. While every attempt was made to consider the most compelling items relevant to their story, not every source, whether primary or secondary, was included. The following, fantastic anecdote—one that could not be corroborated with primary sources—serves as a final example of the mythology (sometimes spurious) surrounding Lincoln and Greeley that does not always belong in a biography. According to a handful of secondary accounts, Lincoln, in the closing days of the war, had told New York Republican assembly speaker George G. Hoskins that the *Tribune*'s support for the Union had been of as much value to him as a division of troops and that such service deserved recognition with an appointment to the postmaster general position. Within days of Robert E. Lee's surrender, according to the same accounts, Greeley had by chance encountered Hoskins and, aware of the conversation, reminded Hoskins that he had heard nothing from Washington about the position. On a Friday evening,

April 14, 1865, Hoskins, fearing his word was in jeopardy, boarded a train to bring the matter to Lincoln's attention. By the time he arrived in Washington, Lincoln was dead.[20]

In at least one rendition of the events that followed, written by *Boston Daily Advertiser* editor Edward Everett Hale (nephew of Edward Everett, the speaker who preceded Lincoln at Gettysburg), Greeley, again feeling the sting of betrayal, had written a scathing column about Lincoln and that night sent the copy to the composing room in the *Tribune* office. Greeley then went home and left managing editor Sidney Gay in charge of the newspaper. Later that night, with the vengeful editorial set to print in the next morning's paper, Gay received word of the president's assassination and spiked the piece. This same account includes an incredible description of the aftermath in the *Tribune* office the next day. Greeley, according to Hale, upon reading his newspaper without the editorial he had written the night before, allegedly called Gay to his office and asked, angrily, "Is it your paper or mine? I should like to know if I cannot print what I choose in my own newspaper!" Gay responded, "The paper is yours, Mr. Greeley. The article is in type upstairs, and you can use it when you choose. Only this, Mr. Greeley: I know New York, and I hope and believe, before God, that there is so much virtue in New York that, if I had let that article go into this morning's paper, there would not be one brick upon another in the *Tribune* office now. Certainly I should be sorry if there were."[21] A later description of events by biographer Harlan Hoyt Horner referred to it as "an ugly story, which has never been substantiated conclusively."[22] Horner makes a sound analysis inasmuch as the events of April 14—or, for that matter, of the entire month of April—do not correspond with what was clearly a mellowing in Greeley's attitudes toward Lincoln. The fairest assessments of Greeley's reaction to the president's death come from respectful eulogies published in the *Tribune*, and if Greeley himself didn't write them, they certainly had Greeley's approval as arbiter of the newspaper's content.[23]

In order to avoid problems in historical interpretation such as the one described, it was essential for me to revisit primary sources, including speeches, newspaper articles, personal letters, and a range of artifacts from the lives of both men. Among the sources cited in this text, Lincoln's personal letters and private papers were available online through archives at the Library of Congress.[24] Duke University provided photocopies of Greeley's private papers, while the University of Rochester made available through microfilm the collection of Thurlow Weed, an influential figure in the careers of both Lincoln and Greeley. *New York Tribune* articles were scoured for key names and events featured in editorials and news stories. Likewise, the online collections of articles from the *Chicago Tribune* and the *New York Times* were reviewed for content related to Lincoln's ascent in the national memory.

NOTES

Preface

1. Emery, Emery, and Roberts, *The Press and America*, 105.

Introduction: Abraham Lincoln and Horace Greeley Remembered

1. Hall, Wentworth, Smith, Greeley, and Weed, *Chicago River and Harbor Convention*, 81, 138, 141.
2. *Chicago Journal*, July 6, 1847; Burlingame, *Abraham Lincoln*, 1:248.
3. *New York Tribune*, July 17, 1847; Horner, *Lincoln and Greeley*, 1–2.
4. *Chicago Journal*, July 6, 1847.
5. Greeley, *Recollections*, 246; Hall, Wentworth, Smith, Greeley, and Weed, *Chicago River and Harbor Convention*, 138.
6. Weed, *Life of Thurlow Weed*, 1:148.
7. In a speech to the U.S. Senate, Clay said, "In Kentucky, almost every manufactory known to me, is in the hands of enterprising and self-made men, who have acquired whatever wealth they possess by patient and diligent labor." Clay, "The American System" (1832), *Works*, 7:464. The phrase "self-made men" (or "the self-made man") later became associated with Clay's political philosophy.
8. Lincoln, "Annual Message to Congress," December 1, 1862, in Basler, *Collected Works*, 5:537; White, *A. Lincoln*, 6.
9. *A Memorial of Horace Greeley*, 76.

1. Self-Made Men

1. Clay, "The American System" (1832), in *Works*, 7:464.
2. Howe, *What Hath God Wrought*, 570–612.
3. Lincoln to Fell, "Enclosing Autobiography," December 20, 1859, in Basler, *Collected Works* (hereafter simply *Collected Works*), 3:511–12; Fehrenbacher, *Lincoln . . . 1859–1865*, 106–8.
4. Scripps to Herndon, June 24, 1865, in Wilson and Davis, *Herndon's Informants*, 57.
5. Lincoln, "Speech in U.S. House of Representatives on the Presidential Question," July 27, 1848, in *Collected Works*, 1:510; Herndon and Weik, *Herndon's Lincoln*, 2:290; Wilson and Davis, *Herndon's Lincoln*, 183.
6. Lincoln, "The House Divided Speech," June 16, 1858, in *Collected Works*, 2:461–69; Miller, *Life and Works*, 3:35–46.
7. Lincoln to Pierce, April 6, 1859, in *Collected Works*, 3:374–76.
8. Barrett, *Life of Abraham Lincoln*, 51–61.
9. Lincoln, "Address before the Young Men's Lyceum," January 27, 1838, in *Collected Works*, 1:108–15.

10. *New York Tribune*, August 5, 1845, May 2, 1846; Commons, "Horace Greeley," 473, 482.
11. Parton, *Life of Horace Greeley* (1855), 250–51.
12. *New York Tribune*, February 29, 1860.
13. Ralph Hoyt, "Personal Reminiscences of Abraham Lincoln," unidentified clipping (April 15, 1900), Lincoln Shrine, A. K. Smiley Public Library, Redlands, California, in Burlingame, *Abraham Lincoln*, 1:124.
14. Lincoln, "To the Editor of the *Sangamo Journal*," June 13, 1836, in *Collected Works*, 1:48; Harper, *Lincoln and the Press*, 1.
15. "Brady on Rail-Splitting," *New York Tribune*, October 23, 1860.
16. Parton, *Life of Horace Greeley* (1855), 2.
17. Ibid., 199–200.
18. March to Richelieu, May 13, 1846, Horace Greeley Papers; Parton, *Life of Horace Greeley* (1855), 201, 202, 217; Isley, *Horace Greeley*, 23; Borchard, "From Pink Lemonade to Salt River."
19. Noyes, *History of American Socialisms*, 10–12, 201, 227, 653; Isley, *Horace Greeley*, 24.
20. Borchard, "Firm of Greeley, Weed, and Seward," 151–55; Bancroft, *Life of William H. Seward*, 1:372; Hudson, *Journalism*, 529, 549; Van Deusen, *Horace Greeley*, 249–53; Van Deusen, *Thurlow Weed*, 97, 201; Van Deusen, *William Henry Seward*, 251; Greeley, *Recollections*, 311–22; Weed, *Life of Thurlow Weed*, 2:554; Williams, *Horace Greeley*, 175.
21. Gillespie to Herndon, January 31, 1866, in Wilson and Davis, *Herndon's Informants*, 181.
22. Fischer, *Tippecanoe*, 29–31.
23. "Campaign Circular from Whig Committee," January [31?], 1840, in *Collected Works*, 1:203; Horner, *Lincoln and Greeley*, 7.
24. Lincoln to Stuart, March 1, 1840, in *Collected Works*, 1:206.
25. "The Log-Cabin Candidate," *Log Cabin*, May 2, 1840.
26. Seward, "To General William Henry Harrison," March 31, 1840, in *Works of William H. Seward*, 3:381–82.
27. "What is the Prospect?" *Log Cabin*, October 31, 1840; "The Work is Done!" *Log Cabin*, November 9, 1840.
28. Holt, *Rise and Fall*, 106.
29. Ingersoll, *Life of Horace Greeley*, 179–81.
30. Commons, "Horace Greeley," 472.
31. "Gen. Harrison at Washington," *Log Cabin*, February 13, 1841; "The Inauguration," ibid., March 13, 1841.
32. "Death of President Harrison!" ibid., April 10, 1841.
33. Greeley, *Recollections*, 136.
34. Parton, *Life of Horace Greeley* (1855), 281; Hudson, *Journalism*, 529; Perry, *Bohemian Brigade*, 49.

35. Howe, *What Hath God Wrought*, 7.
36. Lincoln, "Fragment on Government," July 1, 1854[?], in *Collected Works*, 2:220–21.
37. *New York Tribune*, June 2, 1848; Burlingame, *Abraham Lincoln*, 1:72.
38. Parton, *Life of Horace Greeley* (1855), 248; "Our Defeat in New York," *New York Tribune*, November 11, 1844; Borchard, "*New York Tribune* and the 1844 Election."
39. Parton, *Life of Horace Greeley* (1855), 199–202; Greeley, *Recollections*, 289.

2. Thirtieth Congressmen

1. Lincoln to Mary Lincoln, June 12, 1848, in Basler, *Collected Works* (hereafter simply *Collected Works*), 1:477.
2. Greeley to Weed, January 31, 1848, Weed Papers.
3. Lincoln to Herndon, December 13, 1847, in *Collected Works*, 1:419–20; Miller, *Life and Works*, 8:106.
4. Lincoln, "Speech in the United States House of Representatives," January 12, 1848, in *Collected Works*, 1:431–42; Miller, *Life and Works*, 2:119–33.
5. Lincoln, "'Spot Resolutions' in the United States House of Representatives," December 22, 1847, in *Collected Works*, 1:420–22; Riddle, *Congressman Abraham Lincoln*, 33.
6. Lincoln, "Speech in the United States House of Representatives"; Miller, *Life and Works*, 2:119–33.
7. *Democratic State Register* (Springfield, Ill.), January 21, 28, 1848.
8. Lincoln, "Speech in the United States House of Representatives."
9. "Vote of Thanks to Gen. Taylor," *New York Tribune*, January 5, 1848.
10. Lincoln to Greeley, June 27, 1848, in *Collected Works*, 1:493–92; Miller, *Life and Works*, 8:43–44; "The Boundary of Texas," *New York Tribune*, June 29, 1848.
11. "Lincoln and the Last War and the Next War," *Chicago Tribune*, June 24, 1858; "Mr. Lincoln on the Mexican War," *Chicago Tribune*, July 14, 1858.
12. *New York Herald*, February 11, 1847.
13. Corwin to Greeley, February 21, 1846, Greeley Papers.
14. *New York Tribune*, May 23, August 17, October 18, 1846; Van Deusen, *Horace Greeley*, 109.
15. Greeley, *Hints Toward Reforms*, 354.
16. Greeley and Raymond, *Association Discussed*, preface, 208; *New York Tribune*, April 7, 1853.
17. Greeley, *Recollections*, 216.
18. *New York Tribune*, December 22, 1848.
19. "Land Reform," ibid., December 18, 1848.

20. Greeley, *Recollections*, 217.
21. "Passage of the Homestead Bill," *New York Tribune*, December 6, 1860.
22. Lincoln to Davis, February 12, 1849, in Fehrenbacher, *Lincoln . . . 1832–1858*, 229–30.
23. Lincoln to Herndon, January 8, 1848, in *Collected Works*, 1:30–31; Boritt, "Question of Political Suicide?" 93, 98.
24. Horner, *Lincoln and Greeley*, 51–52.
25. Burlingame, *Abraham Lincoln*, 1:288.
26. Lincoln, "Speech at Peoria, Illinois," October 16, 1854, in *Collected Works*, 2:252.
27. Benton, "Greeley's Estimate of Lincoln," 374.
28. Greeley, *Recollections*, 233; Horner, *Lincoln and Greeley*, 33.
29. Wilson and Davis, *Herndon's Lincoln*, 176; Boritt, "Question of Political Suicide?" 79–100; Neely, "Lincoln and the Mexican War."
30. Horner, *Lincoln and Greeley*, 9, 10.
31. Greeley, *Recollections*, 200, 211.
32. Greeley to Weed, August 17, 1847, Weed Papers; Weed, *Life of Thurlow Weed*, 2:169, 215; Parton, *Life of Horace Greeley* (1855), 286.
33. Faust, *German Element*, 2:360–76; Borchard, "Revolutions Incomplete."
34. "German Whig Rally," *New York Tribune*, November 1, 1848.
35. "Spread of Slavery," ibid., November 1, 1848.
36. Weed to Hamilton Fish, January 16, 1850, Weed Papers; Rhodes, *History of the United States*, 1:134.
37. Weed, *Life of Thurlow Weed*, 2:146, 184–91, 288.
38. Greeley, *Recollections*, 214, 215.
39. Lincoln, "Eulogy on Zachary Taylor at Chicago, Illinois," July 25, 1850, in *Collected Works*, 2:83–90; Fehrenbacher, *Lincoln . . . 1832–1858*, 253.
40. *New York Tribune*, June 30, 1852.
41. Sargent and Greeley, *Life and Public Services*, 4.
42. Lincoln, "Eulogy on Henry Clay," July 6, 1852, in *Collected Works*, 2:121–32; Miller, *Life and Works*, 2:214.
43. Miller, *Life and Works*, 2:210; *Collected Works*, 2:130.
44. Lincoln, "Autobiography Written for John L. Scripps," June 1860, in *Collected Works*, 4:64; Fehrenbacher, *Lincoln . . . 1859–1865*, 167.

3. Free Soil, Free Labor, Free Speech, Free Men

1. Greeley, *Overland Journey*, 99.
2. Wilson and Davis, *Herndon's Lincoln*, 199–200.
3. Lincoln, "To Andrew Johnston," April 18, 1846, in Basler, *Collected Works* (hereafter simply *Collected Works*), 1:377–79; Fehrenbacher, *Lincoln . . . 1832–1858*, 137.

4. Herndon and Weik, *Herndon's Lincoln*, 2:308–9; Wilson and Davis, *Herndon's Lincoln*, 193.

5. Weed, *Life of Thurlow Weed*, 2:214.

6. "Brag Is a Good Dog, But Holdfast Is Better," *New York Tribune*, October 29, 1852; "Another Grand Whig Rally," *New York Tribune*, October 29, 1852; *Boston Pilot*, October 30, 1852, quoted in "The Result and Its Issues," *New York Tribune*, November 4, 1852.

7. Greeley, *Why I Am a Whig*, 3, 5, 15, 16; Borchard, "From Pink Lemonade to Salt River."

8. "Party Names and Public Duty," *New York Tribune*, June 16, 1854; Alexander, *Political History*, 2:205–21.

9. Lincoln, "Speech at Peoria, Illinois," October 16, 1854, in *Collected Works*, 2:247–83; Lehrman, *Lincoln at Peoria*, 215, 239.

10. Lincoln, "Speech at Peoria, Illinois," in *Collected Works*, 2:282.

11. Lincoln to Speed, August 24, 1855, in ibid., 2:322–23.

12. Burlingame, *Abraham Lincoln*, 1:390–403.

13. Lincoln to Speed, August 24, 1855, in *Collected Works*, 2:320–23; Miller, *Life and Works*, 9:190–5.

14. *Philadelphia Public Ledger*, June 20, 1856.

15. Greeley, *Recollections*, 315–21.

16. Lincoln, "Speech at a Republican Banquet, Chicago Illinois," December 10, 1856, in *Collected Works*, 2:383–85; Lehrman, *Lincoln at Peoria*, 184.

17. Guelzo, *Lincoln and Douglas*, 1.

18. White, *A. Lincoln*, 264.

19. "Fourth Debate with Stephen A. Douglas at Charleston, Illinois," September 18, 1858, in *Collected Works*, 3:145–201; Guelzo, *Lincoln and Douglas*, 191–98

20. Lincoln, "The Galesburg Debate," Galesburg, Illinois, October 7, 1858, in *Collected Works*, 3:207–44; Miller, *Life and Works*, 4:36–85.

21. "O! Come Back Stephen," *Chicago Tribune*, August 19, 1858; White, *A. Lincoln*, 270.

22. Herndon to Theodore Parker, November 8, 1858, in Newton, *Lincoln and Herndon*, 231–32, 234–35; Guelzo, *Lincoln and Douglas*, 288.

23. Parton, *Life of Horace Greeley* (1872), 252; Guelzo, *Lincoln and Douglas*, 48.

24. Davis to Lincoln, November 7, 1858, and Judd to Lincoln, October 20, 1859, *Abraham Lincoln Papers*.

25. Herndon to Lincoln, March 24, 1858, in Wilson and Davis, *Herndon's Lincoln*, 242.

26. Lincoln, "Speech at Columbus, Ohio," September 16, 1859, in *Collected Works*, 3:402.

27. Lincoln to Kellogg, December 11, 1859, in ibid., 3:506–7; Fehrenbacher, *Lincoln . . . 1859–1865*, 102.

28. Lincoln to Trumbull, December 28, 1857, in *Collected Works*, 2:430; Fehrenbacher, *Lincoln . . . 1832–1858*, 419.

29. Wilson and Davis, *Herndon's Lincoln*, 239; Lincoln to Herndon, in Fehrenbacher and Fehrenbacher, *Recollected Words*, 250.

30. Wentworth to Lincoln, April 19, 1858, *Abraham Lincoln Papers*.

31. *New York Herald*, October 8–24, 27–31, November 1–8, December 2, 1859.

32. "John Brown Dead," *New York Tribune*, December 3, 1859; Borchard, "*New York Tribune* at Harper's Ferry."

33. "Letter from Theodore Parker," *New York Tribune*, December 27, 1859.

34. "What Is Asked of Republicans?" *Montgomery Mail*, quoted in ibid., December 31, 1860.

35. Holzer, *Lincoln at Cooper Union*, 6.

36. Lincoln, "Address at Cooper Institute, New York City," February 27, 1860, in *Collected Works*, 3:550; Holzer, *Lincoln at Cooper Union*, 143.

37. Lincoln, "Address at Cooper Institute, New York City," February 27, 1860, in *Collected Works*, 3:522–50.

38. Holzer, *Lincoln at Cooper Union*, 106; Donald and Holzer, *Lincoln in the Times*, 18.

39. Holzer, *Lincoln at Cooper Union*, 178.

40. *New York Tribune*, February 28, 1860.

41. "Mr. Lincoln's Speeches," *Chicago Tribune*, March 2, 1860.

42. F. Curtis, *Republican Party*, 2:498.

43. Carey, *History of Oregon*, 635.

44. "A Card by Greeley," *New York Tribune*, February 20, 1860.

45. Weed, *Life of Thurlow Weed*, 2:269.

46. Bartlett, *Life and Public Services*, 109; Coffin, *Abraham Lincoln*, 188.

47. Nicolay and Hay, *Abraham Lincoln: A History*, 2:265–77; Browne, *Everyday Life*, 232–33.

48. Butler to Lincoln, May 15, 1860, *Abraham Lincoln Papers*.

49. Herndon and Weik, *Herndon's Lincoln*, 3:462; Wilson and Davis, *Herndon's Lincoln*, 278.

50. Butler to Lincoln, May 16, 1860, *Abraham Lincoln Papers*.

51. Weed, *Life of Thurlow Weed*, 2:269.

52. Greeley, *Recollections*, 390–91.

53. Herndon and Weik, *Herndon's Lincoln*, 3:461–62.

54. Bancroft, *Life of William H. Seward*, 1:524–40.

55. Greeley, *Recollections*, 315–21.

56. Weed, *Life of Thurlow Weed*, 2:250, 261–71.

57. "Horace Greeley's Letter," *New York Times*, June 15, 1860.

58. "Political Intelligence," *New York Tribune*, June 3, 1860.

59. Seward to Lincoln, October 8, 1860, *Abraham Lincoln Papers*.

4. A Fight for Union and for Freedom

1. Lincoln, "Autobiography Written for John L. Scripps," June 1860, in Basler, *Collected Works* (hereafter simply *Collected Works*), 4:60–67; Burlingame, *Abraham Lincoln*, 1:648.

2. Nicolay, *Short Life*, 156–57.

3. "Republican Central Campaign Club," *New York Tribune*, June 1, 1860.

4. Ibid., November 8, 1860.

5. "The Political Text-Book for 1860," ibid., September 11, 1860; Greeley, *Political Text-Book*, 72.

6. "Fused at Last," *New York Tribune*, September 10, 1860; "Playing Possum," ibid., October 1, 1860; "After the Election," ibid., November 6, 1860.

7. "The Republicans of the Slave States," ibid., October 12, 1860.

8. *New York Herald*, November 5, 1860.

9. "The Republican Jubilee," *New York Tribune*, November 9, 1860.

10. Lincoln to Hodges, April 4, 1864, in *Collected Works*, 7:282.

11. Medill to Lincoln, July 5, 1860, *Abraham Lincoln Papers*.

12. Forney to Lincoln, November 12, 1860, ibid.

13. Lincoln in Fehrenbacher and Fehrenbacher, *Recollected Words*, 264.

14. Lincoln to Weed, February 4, 1861, in *Collected Works*, 4:185–86; Fehrenbacher, *Lincoln . . . 1859–1865*, 198; "From Springfield, Mr. Greeley and His Senatorial Defeat," *Chicago Tribune*, February 5, 1861.

15. "Are We Going to Fight," *New York Tribune,* November 30, 1860.

16. "The Right of Secession," ibid., December 17, 1860.

17. "No Compromise!" ibid., February 18 to February 28, 1861.

18. Burlingame, *Abraham Lincoln*, 2:126, 179; Williams, *Horace Greeley*, 227.

19. Raymond to Lincoln, November 14, 1860, *Abraham Lincoln Papers*.

20. *New York Tribune*, April 15, 1861.

21. "The Nation's War-Cry," ibid., June 26 to July 4, 1861.

22. "The Latest War News," ibid., July 23, 1861.

23. "Just Once," ibid., July 24, 1861.

24. Greeley to Conway, August 17, 1861, in Conway, *Autobiography*, 1:298; Burlingame, *Abraham Lincoln*, 2:185.

25. Greeley to Lincoln, July 29, 1861, *Abraham Lincoln Papers*.

26. Fehrenbacher and Fehrenbacher, *Recollected Words*, 224.

27. "Reply to Emancipation Memorial Presented by Chicago Christians of All Denominations," September 13, 1862, in *Collected Works*, 5:421; Fehrenbacher, *Lincoln . . . 1859–1865*, 362.

28. Fehrenbacher and Fehrenbacher, *Recollected Words*, 123.

29. Guelzo, *Abraham Lincoln*, 198–99.

30. Sherman to Draper, March 15, 1870, in Hirshson, *White Tecumseh*, 289.

31. Lincoln to Hodges, April 4, 1864, in *Collected Works*, 7:282.
32. Lincoln to Greeley, March 24, 1862, in ibid., 5:169; Fehrenbacher, *Lincoln . . . 1859–1865*, 312.
33. Van Deusen, *William Henry Seward*, 333.
34. Guelzo, *Lincoln's Emancipation Proclamation*, 1, 128–30.
35. Burlingame, *Abraham Lincoln*, 2:400–404.
36. "The Prayer of Twenty Millions," *New York Tribune*, August 20, 1862; Greeley, *American Conflict*, 2:250.
37. Lincoln to Greeley, August 22, 1862, in *Collected Works*, 5:388–89; Fehrenbacher, *Lincoln . . . 1859–1865*, 358; "Lincoln's Reply to Greeley," *Chicago Tribune*, August 25, 1862.
38. Hill to Gay, September 1, 1862, Gay Papers, in Fehrenbacher and Fehrenbacher, *Recollected Words*, 18.
39. Guelzo, *Abraham Lincoln*, 139–40.
40. Guelzo, *Lincoln's Emancipation Proclamation*, 136.
41. *New York Tribune*, August 24, 1862; Guelzo, *Lincoln's Emancipation Proclamation*, 136–37.
42. *New York Tribune*, September 23, 1863.
43. Fehrenbacher and Fehrenbacher, *Recollected Words*, 182.
44. Lincoln to James C. Conkling, August 26, 1863, in *Collected Works*, 6:409.
45. Lincoln, "Announcement of News from Gettysburg," July 4, 1863, in ibid., 6:314; see Lincoln's letters to Lee, Schenck, French, Halleck, Welles, Low, Smith, Thomas, Sickles, Dubois, Stanton, Wright, Grant, Schofield, and Meade in ibid., 6:314–29.
46. *New York Herald*, July 4, 6, 7, 1863; *New York Times*, July 3, 6, 1863.
47. *New York Tribune*, July 4, 6, 8, 1863.
48. Ibid., March 8, 1862.
49. Ibid., July 8, 1863; Lincoln, "Response to a Serenade," July 7, 1863, in *Collected Works*, 6:319–20.
50. Information from the Gettysburg National Military Park website, "Frequently Asked Questions" page.
51. Elmore, *Lincoln's Gettysburg Address*, 126–28.
52. *Chicago Times*, November 22, 1863; "The Heroes of July," *New York Times*, November 20, 1863.
53. Greeley to Jewett, January 2, 1863, in Parton, *Life of Horace Greeley* (1872), 469.
54. "Opening the Presidential Campaign," *New York Tribune*, February 23, 1864.
55. *New York Tribune*, March 20, 1864; Burlingame, *Abraham Lincoln*, 2:633.
56. Greeley to Opdyke, August 18, 1864, *New York Sun*, June 30, 1889, in Alexander, *Political History*, 3:104; Horner, *Lincoln and Greeley*, 351.
57. *New York Tribune*, September 6, 1864.

58. Cullom, *Fifty Years*, 101.
59. Fehrenbacher and Fehrenbacher, *Recollected Words*, 19, 182; Ashley, *Address of Hon. J. M. Ashley*, 13; Burlingame, *Abraham Lincoln*, 2:670.
60. Lincoln to Greeley, July 9, 1864, in *Collected Works*, 7:435–36; Fehrenbacher, *Lincoln . . . 1859–1865*, 606.
61. Greeley, *American Conflict*, 2:664.
62. Lincoln to Greeley, July 15, 1864, in *Collected Works*, 7:440–42; Fehrenbacher, *Lincoln . . . 1859–1865*, 608.
63. Zabriskie, *Horace Greeley*, 252–56.
64. Lincoln to Greeley, August 6, 1864, in *Collected Works*, 7:482–83; Nicolay and Hay, *Abraham Lincoln: Complete Works*, 2:559.
65. Lincoln to Greeley, August 9, 1864, in *Collected Works*, 7:489–90; Fehrenbacher, *Lincoln . . . 1859–1865*, 618.
66. Lincoln to Raymond, August 15, 1864, in *Collected Works*, 7:494–95; Fehrenbacher, *Lincoln . . . 1859–1865*, 619.
67. W. Curtis, *Abraham Lincoln*, 284.
68. Welles, *Diary of Gideon Welles*, 2:112; Fehrenbacher and Fehrenbacher, *Recollected Words*, 138, 483.
69. Donald, *Lincoln*, 414; Isley, *Horace Greeley*, 334.
70. "Greeley vs. Lincoln," *Chicago Tribune*, August 15, 1865.
71. "The President's Health," *New York Tribune*, March 17, 1865.

Conclusion: Re-remembering Lincoln and Greeley

1. *New York Tribune*, April 10, 1865.
2. Herndon interview of Lamon, in Wilson and Davis, *Herndon's Informants*, 466.
3. Arnold, *Life of Abraham Lincoln*, 429–30.
4. *New York Tribune*, April 18, 19, 1865.
5. Benton, "Greeley's Estimate of Lincoln," 371; Benton, *Greeley on Lincoln*, 12; Horner, *Lincoln and Greeley*, 390.
6. *New York World*, June 20, 1864; April 17, 1865.
7. *Assassination of Abraham Lincoln*, 1–717; Harper, *Lincoln and the Press*, 360–62.
8. *New York Herald*, April 16, 1865.
9. Truman, "Anecdotes of Andrew Johnson," 439.
10. "A Card," *New York Tribune*, May 3, 1865.
11. "H. G. and A. L.," *Chicago Tribune*, February 9, 1869.
12. "Mr. Greeley for Senator," ibid., November 17, 1866.
13. Parton, *Life of Horace Greeley* (1872), 539–42.
14. Greeley, *Recollections*, 390.
15. Greeley, "Greeley's Estimate of Lincoln," 14–15; Benton, *Greeley on Lincoln*, 6; Benton, "Greeley's Estimate of Lincoln," 371; "Open Letters."

16. Greeley, "Greeley's Estimate of Lincoln," 31; Benton, "Greeley's Estimate of Lincoln," 382.
17. Benton, *Greeley on Lincoln*, 25.
18. Borchard, "Taking No Rights For Granted."
19. Van Deusen, *Horace Greeley*, 386–87.
20. "Mr. Greeley and the Democratic New Departure," *Chicago Tribune*, June 22, 1871.
21. Pearson, "*Tribune* Endorsing Obama, Backing of Democrat for President a First," ibid., October 18, 2008.
22. *New York Tribune*, May 22, 1872; Van Deusen, *Horace Greeley*, 408.
23. Rhodes, *History of the United States*, 7:13.
24. Alexander, *Political History*, 3:301; Bancroft, *Life of William H. Seward*, 2:525; Weed, *Life of Thurlow Weed*, 1:467, 2:283–84, 576.
25. *A Memorial of Horace Greeley*, 21; "Greeley's Statement," Greeley Papers, November 13, 1872; Van Deusen, *Horace Greeley*, 424.
26. Parton, *Life of Horace Greeley* (1855), 441–42.
27. Van Deusen, *Horace Greeley*, 424.
28. Cuyler, "Uncle Horace."
29. Holden, *Proceedings at the Unveiling*, 54.
30. "First Debate with Stephen A. Douglas at Ottawa, Illinois," August, 21, 1858, in Basler, *Collected Works*, 3:29; Nicolay and Hay, *Abraham Lincoln: Complete Works*, 1:299; Lincoln to Fell, "Enclosing Autobiography," December 20, 1859, in *Collected Works*, 3:511–12; Fehrenbacher, *Lincoln . . . 1859–1865*, 108.
31. Greeley, *Recollections*, 166.
32. "Harding Dedicates Lincoln Memorial," *New York Times*, May 31, 1922.
33. Clay and Mallory, "In Defense of the American System," *Life and Speeches*, 2:5–55.

Notes on Sources

1. Wilson and Davis, *Herndon's Lincoln*, xv; Parton, *Life of Horace Greeley* (1872), 539–48.
2. Beran, *Forge of Empires*, 7.
3. Lincoln, "Autobiography Written for John L. Scripps," June 1860, in Basler, *Collected Works* (hereafter simply *Collected Works*), 4:60–67; Kaplan, *Lincoln*, 315–16.
4. Williams, *Horace Greeley*, 125–42.
5. Commons, "Horace Greeley," 472; Tuchinsky, *Horace Greeley's New-York Tribune*, 13–17.
6. *Harper's Weekly*, September 15, 1860.
7. *New York Herald*, April 20, 1841.
8. Beveridge, *Abraham Lincoln*, 2:127–28, 171, 185.

9. Randall and Current, *Lincoln the President*, 1:138, 2:63, 204, 218, 221.
10. Ibid., 4:154, 266.
11. Bulla, *Lincoln's Censor*, 8, 68, 112; Weber, *Copperheads*, 73–102.
12. Neely, *Fate of Liberty*, 12–13.
13. Lincoln to Hodges, April 4, 1864, *Collected Works*, 7:282; Donald, *Lincoln*, frontispiece.
14. Shenk, *Lincoln's Melancholy*, 11.
15. Linn, *Horace Greeley*, 192.
16. Williams, *Horace Greeley*, 10.
17. Perry, *Bohemian Brigade*, 47.
18. Jack Canfield and Mark Victor Hansen, "Abraham Lincoln Didn't Quit," *Chicken Soup for the Soul: 101 Stories to Open the Heart and Rekindle the Spirit* (Deerfield Beach, Fla.: Health Communications, 1993), 229, 230; "The Glurge of Springfield," available at http://www.snopes.com/glurge/lincoln.asp, accessed March 1, 2010.
19. Parton, *Life of Horace Greeley* (1855), 414; Greeley, *Recollections*, 360–89.
20. Hale, *Horace Greeley*, 288, 289; Harper, *Lincoln and the Press*, 347.
21. Hale, *James Russell Lowell*, 178–79.
22. Horner, *Lincoln and Greeley*, 382.
23. "The Dawn of Peace," *New York Tribune*, April 14, 1865.
24. *Abraham Lincoln Papers*.

SELECTED BIBLIOGRAPHY

Primary Sources

Abraham Lincoln Papers at the Library of Congress. Manuscript Division. Washington, D.C.: American Memory Project, 2000–02. http://memory .loc.gov/ammem/alhtml/alhome.html, accessed March 1, 2010.

Alexander, DeAlva Stanwood. *A Political History of the State of New York.* 3 vols. New York: Henry Holt and Co., 1909.

Arnold, Isaac N. *The Life of Abraham Lincoln.* Chicago: Jansen, McClurg and Company, 1885.

Ashley, James Mitchell. *Address of Hon. J. M. Ashley at the Fourth Annual Banquet of the Ohio Republican League.* New York: Evening Post, 1891.

The Assassination of Abraham Lincoln. Washington: Government Printing Office, 1866.

Bancroft, Frederic. *The Life of William H. Seward.* 2 vols. New York: Harper and Brothers, 1900.

Barrett, Joseph H. *Life of Abraham Lincoln.* Cincinnati: Moore, Wilstach, Baldwin, 1864.

Bartlett, D. W., and Abraham Lincoln. *The Life and Public Services of Hon. Abraham Lincoln.* New York: H. Dayton, 1860.

Basler, Roy P., ed. *The Collected Works of Abraham Lincoln.* 9 vols. New Brunswick, N.J.: Rutgers University Press, 1953–55.

Benton, Joel. *Greeley on Lincoln.* New York: Baker and Taylor Company, 1893.

———. "Greeley's Estimate of Lincoln." *Century: A Popular Quarterly* 42.3 (July 1891): 371–83.

Browne, Francis Fisher. *The Every-day Life of Abraham Lincoln.* Chicago: Brown and Howell, 1913.

Carey, Charles H. *History of Oregon.* Chicago and Portland: Pioneer Historical Publishing, 1922.

Clay, Henry. *Works.* Edited by Calvin Colton. 10 vols. New York: G. P. Putnam's Sons, 1904.

Clay, Henry, and Daniel Mallory. *The Life and Speeches of Henry Clay.* 2 vols. New York: A. S. Barnes and Company, 1857.

Coffin, Charles Carleton. *Abraham Lincoln.* New York: Harper and Brothers, 1893.

Conway, Moncure Daniel. *Autobiography, Memories and Experiences of Moncure Daniel Conway.* 2 vols. Boston and New York: Houghton, Mifflin and Company, 1905.

Cullom, Shelby M. *Fifty Years of Public Service: Personal Recollections of Shelby M. Cullom*. Chicago: McClurg, 1911.

Curtis, Francis. *The Republican Party: A History of Its Fifty Years' Existence*. 2 vols. New York: G. P. Putnam, 1904.

Curtis, William Eleroy. *Abraham Lincoln*. Philadelphia: J. B. Lippincott Company, 1902.

Cuyler, Theodore H. "Uncle Horace." *Temperance Record* 877 (January 25, 1873): 40.

Faust, Albert Bernhardt. *German Element in the United States*. 2 vols. Boston and New York: Houghton Mifflin Company, 1909.

Fehrenbacher, Don E., ed. *Lincoln: Speeches and Writings, 1832–1858*. New York: Library of America, 1989.

———. *Lincoln: Speeches and Writings, 1859–1865*. New York: Library of America, 1989.

Fehrenbacher, Don E., and Virginia Fehrenbacher, eds. *Recollected Words of Abraham Lincoln*. Stanford, Calif.: Stanford University Press, 1996.

Greeley, Horace. *The American Conflict*. 2 vols. New York: O. D. Case, 1864, 1866.

———. "Greeley's Estimate of Lincoln." Hancock, N.Y.: Herald Printery, unpublished (1868?).

———. *Hints Toward Reforms, in Lectures, Addresses, and Other Writings*. New York: Harper, 1850.

———. *An Overland Journey from New York to San Francisco in the Summer of 1859*. New York: C. M. Saxton, Barker and Co., 1860.

———. Papers. Duke University, Durham, N.C. Rare Book, Manuscript, and Special Collections Library. Call Number or Mss. Loc: 6th 17:B, uncat. coll. boxes.

———. *A Political Text-Book for 1860*. New York: Tribune Association, 1860.

———. *Recollections of a Busy Life*. New York: J. B. Ford, 1868.

———. *Why I Am a Whig*. New York: Tribune Office, 1852.

Greeley, Horace, and Henry Jarvis Raymond. *Association Discussed; or, The Socialism of the Tribune Examined*. New York: Harper, 1847.

Hale, Edward Everett. *James Russell Lowell and His Friends, by Edward Everett Hale*. Boston and New York: Houghton, Mifflin and Company, 1899.

Hall, William Mosley, John Wentworth, Samuel Lisle Smith, Horace Greeley, and Thurlow Weed. *Chicago River and Harbor Convention: An Account of Its Origin and Proceedings*. Chicago: Fergus Printing Company, 1882.

Herndon, William Henry, and Jesse William Weik. *Herndon's Lincoln: The True Story of a Great Life*. 3 vols. Chicago: Belford-Clarke, 1890.

Holden, James Austin, ed. *Proceedings at the Unveiling of a Memorial to Horace Greeley at Chappaqua, N.Y., February 3, 1914*. Albany: University of the State of New York, 1915.

Hudson, Frederic. *Journalism in the United States, from 1690 to 1872*. New York: Harper Brothers, 1873.

Ingersoll, Lurton Dunham. *The Life of Horace Greeley: Founder of the New York Tribune*. Chicago: Union Publishing, 1873.

Linn, William Alexander. *Horace Greeley, Founder and Editor of the New York Tribune*. New York: D. Appleton, 1908.

A Memorial of Horace Greeley. New York: Tribune Association, 1873.

Miller, Marion Mills, ed. *Life and Works of Abraham Lincoln*. 9 vols. New York: Current Literature Publishing, 1907.

Newton, Joseph Fort. *Lincoln and Herndon*. Cedar Rapids, Iowa: Torch Press, 1910.

Nicolay, John G. *A Short Life of Abraham Lincoln*. New York: Century, 1917.

Nicolay, John G., and John Hay. *Abraham Lincoln: A History*. 10 vols. New York: Century, 1890.

———. *Abraham Lincoln: Complete Works*. 2 vols. New York: Century, 1894.

Noyes, John Humphrey. *History of American Socialisms*. Philadelphia: J. B. Lippincott, 1870. Reprint, New York: Dover, 1966.

"Open Letters." *Century* (September 1891): 798.

Parton, James. *The Life of Horace Greeley*. New York: Mason Brothers, 1855.

———. *The Life of Horace Greeley, Editor of the New York Tribune, From His Birth to the Present Time*. Boston: James R. Osgood and Company, 1872.

Rhodes, James Ford. *History of the United States from the Compromise of 1850*. 8 vols. New York: Harper and Brothers, 1899.

Sargent, Epes, and Horace Greeley. *The Life and Public Services of Henry Clay*. New York: C. M. Saxton, 1852, 1860.

Seward, William H. *The Works of William H. Seward*. Ed. George E. Baker. 5 vols. Boston and New York: Houghton, Mifflin and Company, 1884.

Truman, Benjamin C. "Anecdotes of Andrew Johnson." *Century Magazine* 85.3 (January 1913): 435–40.

Weed, Thurlow. *Life of Thurlow Weed Including His Autobiography and a Memoir*. 2 vols. Boston and New York: Houghton, Mifflin and Company, 1883–84.

———. Papers, 1846–58 (microfilm). Rochester. New York Historical Society.

Welles, Gideon. *The Diary of Gideon Welles*. 3 vols. Boston: Houghton Mifflin, 1911.

Wilson, Douglas L., and Rodney O. Davis, eds. *Herndon's Informants: Letters, Interviews, and Statements about Abraham Lincoln*. Urbana: University of Illinois Press, 1998.

———. *Herndon's Lincoln*. Urbana: University of Illinois Press, 2006.

Zabriskie, Francis Nicoll. *Horace Greeley, the Editor*. New York: Funk and Wagnalls, 1890.

Newspapers

Chicago Journal
Chicago Times
Chicago Tribune
Democratic State Register, Springfield, Ill.
Log Cabin
New York Herald
New York Times
New York Tribune
New York World
Philadelphia Public Ledger

Secondary Sources

Beran, Michael Knox. *Forge of Empires*. New York: Free Press, 2007.

Beveridge, Albert J. *Abraham Lincoln, 1809–1858*. 2 vols. New York: Houghton Mifflin, 1928.

Borchard, Gregory A. "The Firm of Greeley, Weed, and Seward: New York Partisanship and the Press, 1840–1860." Ph.D. diss., University of Florida, 2003.

———. "From Pink Lemonade to Salt River: Horace Greeley's Utopia and the Death of the Whig Party." *Journalism History* 32.1 (Spring 2006): 22–33.

———. "*The New York Tribune* and the 1844 Election: Horace Greeley, Gangs, and the Wise Men of Gotham." *Journalism History* 33.1 (Spring 2007): 51–59.

———. "*The New York Tribune* at Harper's Ferry: Horace Greeley on Trial." *American Journalism* 20.1 (Winter 2003): 13–31.

———. "Revolutions Incomplete: Horace Greeley and the Forty-eighters at Home and Abroad." *American Journalism* 27.1 (Winter 2010): 7–36.

———. "Taking No Rights For Granted: The Southern Press and the 15th Amendment." In *Words at War*, edited by David B. Sachsman, S. Kittrell Rushing, and Roy Morris Jr., 309–18. West Lafayette, Ind.: Purdue University Press, 2008.

Boritt, Gabor S. "A Question of Political Suicide? Lincoln's Opposition to the Mexican War." *Journal of the Illinois State Historical Society* 67 (February 1974): 79–100.

Bulla, David W. *Lincoln's Censor: Milo Hascall and Freedom of the Press in Civil War Indiana*. West Lafayette, Ind.: Purdue University Press, 2009.

Burlingame, Michael. *Abraham Lincoln: A Life*. 2 vols. Baltimore: Johns Hopkins University Press, 2008.

Commons, John R. "Horace Greeley and the Working Class Origins of the Republican Party." *Political Science Quarterly* 24 (1909): 466–88.

Donald, David Herbert. *Lincoln*. New York: Simon and Schuster, 1995.

Donald, David Herbert, and Harold Holzer. *Lincoln in the* Times*: The Life of Abraham Lincoln as Originally Reported in* The New York Times. New York: St. Martin's, 2005.

Elmore, A. E. *Lincoln's Gettysburg Address: Echoes of the Bible and Book of Common Prayer*. Carbondale: Southern Illinois University Press, 2009.

Emery, Edwin, Michael Emery, and Nancy Roberts. *The Press and America: An Interpretive History of the Mass Media*. 9th ed. Boston: Allyn and Bacon, 2000.

Fischer, Roger A. *Tippecanoe and Trinkets Too: The Material Culture of American Presidential Campaigns, 1828–1984*. Urbana: University of Illinois Press, 1988.

Gettysburg National Military Park. *NPS.gov*. http://www.nps.gov/gett/, accessed March 1, 2011.

Guelzo, Allen C. *Abraham Lincoln as a Man of Ideas*. Carbondale: Southern Illinois University Press, 2009.

———. *Lincoln and Douglas: The Debates that Defined America*. New York: Simon and Schuster, 2008.

———. *Lincoln's Emancipation Proclamation*. New York: Simon and Schuster, 2004.

Hale, William Harlan. *Horace Greeley: Voice of the People*. New York: Harper and Brothers, 1950.

Harper, Robert S. *Lincoln and the Press*. New York: McGraw-Hill, 1951.

Hirshson, Stanley P. *The White Tecumseh: A Biography of General William T. Sherman*. New York: John Wiley, 1997.

Holt, Michael F. *The Rise and Fall of the American Whig Party: Jacksonian Politics and the Onset of the Civil War*. New York: Oxford University Press, 1999.

Holzer, Harold. *Lincoln at Cooper Union: The Speech That Made Abraham Lincoln President*. New York: Simon and Schuster, 2004.

Horner, Harlan Hoyt. *Lincoln and Greeley*. Urbana: University of Illinois Press, 1953.

Howe, Daniel Walker. *What Hath God Wrought: The Transformation of America, 1815–1848*. New York: Oxford University Press, 2007.

Isley, Jeter Allen. *Horace Greeley and the Republican Party*. Princeton, N.J.: Princeton University Press, 1947.

Kaplan, Fred. *Lincoln: The Biography of a Writer*. New York: HarperCollins, 2008.

Lehrman, Lewis E. *Lincoln at Peoria: The Turning Point*. Mechanicsburg, Pa.: Stackpole, 2008.

Neely, Mark E., Jr. *The Fate of Liberty: Abraham Lincoln and Civil Liberties*. Oxford: Oxford University Press, 1991.

———. "Lincoln and the Mexican War: An Argument by Analogy." *Civil War History* 24 (March 1978): 5–24.

Perry, James M. *A Bohemian Brigade: The Civil War Correspondents.* New York: John Wiley, 2000.

Randall, James G., and Richard N. Current. *Lincoln the President.* 4 vols. New York: Dodd, Mead, 1945–55.

Riddle, Donald W. *Congressman Abraham Lincoln.* Urbana: University of Illinois Press, 1957.

Shenk, Joshua Wolf. *Lincoln's Melancholy: How Depression Challenged a President and Fueled His Greatness.* Boston: Houghton Mifflin, 2005.

Tuchinsky, Adam. *Horace Greeley's* New-York Tribune: *Civil War–Era Socialism and the Crisis of Free Labor.* Ithaca: Cornell University Press, 2009.

Van Deusen, Glyndon G. *Horace Greeley, Nineteenth-Century Crusader.* New York: Hill and Wang, 1953.

———. *Thurlow Weed: Wizard of the Lobby.* Boston: Little, Brown, 1947.

———. *William Henry Seward.* New York: Oxford University Press, 1967.

Weber, Jennifer L. *Copperheads: The Rise and Fall of Lincoln's Opponents in the North.* Oxford: Oxford University Press, 2006.

White, Ronald C. *A. Lincoln: A Biography.* New York: Random House, 2009.

Williams, Robert C. *Horace Greeley: Champion of American Freedom.* New York: New York University Press, 2006.

INDEX

Illustrations are indicated by the italicized word *gallery.*

abolitionists, 53, 76, 78–79

Abraham Lincoln, 1809–1858 (Beveridge), 108–9

Abraham Lincoln: A Life (Burlingame), 106

Adams, John Quincy, 6

African Americans, racist notions toward, 13

Age of Clay, 7–8

Age of Jackson, 7

Alger, Horatio, 7

American Conflict, The (Greeley), 94

American System, 2–3, 7, 11, 26

Ames, Dr., at Republican national convention, 63

amnesty for Confederates, 94–95

anti-immigrant sentiments, 52

Army of the Potomac, 81

Ashley, James, 85

Ashmun Amendment, 31

Baltimore Republican (periodical), 20

Bates, Edward, 1, 62, 78

battles: Antietam (Sharpsburg), 79–80; Bull Run, First (Manassas), 74; Gettysburg, 81–83; Osawatomie, Kansas, 53; Vicksburg, 81

Beecher, Henry Ward, 99

Bell, John, 61, 68–69

Bennett, James Gordon: on Battle of Gettysburg, 81; on Greeley, 108; on Lincoln's assassination, 93; as Lincoln supporter, 71, 90–91; ministerial appointment offered by Lincoln, 88; on Polk and Mexican-American War, 32

Beran, Michael Knox, 106

Beveridge, Albert J., 108–9

Birchall, Caleb, 37

Birney, James G., 25–26

Black Hawk War, 8

Blair, Francis, Sr., in *Vanity Fair* cartoon, *gallery*

Blair, Montgomery, 78

Boston Pilot (periodical), 47

Breckinridge, John C., 61, 68–69

Brisbane, Albert, 16–17

Brook Farm, Massachusetts, 17

Brown, John, 53, 58–59

Bryant, William Cullen, 59

Buchanan, James, 52–53, 55

Burlingame, Michael, 106

Butler, William, 63–64

Cameron, Simon, 63–64

Cass, Lewis, 2, 38–39

Chase, Salmon P., 78, 99

Cheney, Mary Y. "Molly," 16

Chicago Journal, on Lincoln, 2

Chicago River and Harbor Convention, 1–2

Chicago Tribune (periodical): on Greeley, 88, 94–95, 97; on Lincoln, 32, 45; in new generation of editors, 28–29

citizen journalism, in *New York Tribune*, 108

civil liberties, Lincoln's management of, 76, 109

Civil War, end of, 90

Clay, Henry: Age of, 7–8; and the American System, 2–3, 7, 11; eulogies for, 41–43; Greeley and Lincoln as leading disciples of, 5, 26, 100–101; presidential campaigns, 23–26, 28, 38; retirement from and return to politics, 39–40; on self-made men, 115n. 7; Whig vision of, 6

Colfax, Schuyler, 1

Commons, John R., 22

communication revolution, 23

Compromise of 1850, 40, 54

Constitutional Union Party, 61
Cooper Union address, 58–59
Corwin, Thomas, 2, 32
Current, Richard N., 109
Cuyler, Theodore H., 99

Dana, Charles A., 74, *gallery*
Davis, David, 63
Davis, Jefferson, 67–68, 95
Dayton, William, 51
Democratic State Register (periodical), 30–31
Democrats and Democratic Party: and 1852 election, 48; Douglas as head of, in Illinois, 19; Greeley as presidential nominee of, 97; Lincoln criticized by newspapers of, 37; Lincoln on principles of, 9; Lincoln's support among, as Union president, 71; national conventions, 60–61; northern, Douglas as presidential candidate of, 61, 68–69; peace platform, 84; pro-annexation (of Texas) candidate and platform, 25; problems within, 38–39
Donald, David Herbert, 110
Douglas, Stephen A.: Beveridge's account of, 109; as Democratic Party head in Illinois, 19; elected to U.S. Senate, 29; Greeley's support for, 44; and Kansas-Nebraska Act, 49–50; in new generation of politicians, 28; popular sovereignty and, 40, 54; presidential campaign of, 61, 67–69; Republican Party and, 55
Dubois, Jesse K., 63–64

economic recession (1858), 53
elections: of 1824, 6; of 1832, 6; of 1844, 7; of 1848, 39; of 1852, 48; of 1858, 53–60; of 1860, 56, 68–70, 107; of 1864, 90
Emancipation Proclamation, 77–80

falsehoods in popular legends, 110–11

Fate of Liberty, The: Abraham Lincoln and Civil Liberties (Neely), 109–10
federal land policy, 34–35
Field, David Dudley, 1, 59
Fillmore, Millard, 33, 41, 47
Firm of Seward, Weed, and Greeley, The, 18, 51–52, 60
First Battle of Bull Run (Manassas), 74
First Party System, as foundation for careers of Lincoln and Greeley, 9
Forge of Empires (Beran), 106
Forney, John W., 71
Fourier, Charles, 16–17
Fourierism, 16–17
Frank Leslie's Illustrated Newspaper, 98, *gallery*
freedom, new birth of, 77–83
free labor principle, 12
Free Soil Party, 48
Frémont, John C., 51–52, 83–84
Fry, William Henry, *gallery*
Fugitive Slave Law, 41
Fuller, Margaret, 22
funeral train, Lincoln's, 93

Gettysburg, Pennsylvania, *gallery*
Gettysburg Address, 83
Giddings, Joshua R., 36
Gilmore, James R., 79
Gott, Daniel, 36–37
Grahamites, 16
Grant, Ulysses S., 4, 81, 90, 96, 98–99
"Great Skedaddle," 74
Greele, Andrew, 5–6
Greeley, Horace: in 30th Congress, 27; ancestors of, 5–6; antislavery editorials, 32–33, 39; on Ashmun Amendment, 31; autobiography of, 95; on Battle of Gettysburg, 81–82; brain fever (nervous breakdown), 74–75, 110; Chicago River and Harbor Convention, 1–2; on Civil War and secession, 72–73; Clay's eulogy, 41–42; Clay's presidential bid and, 24,

26, 28; as Congressman, 34; contradictory statements by, 73; daguerreotype, *gallery*; deterioration, death, and funeral of, 98–99; as Douglas supporter, 55–56; and economic growth in the West, 12; education of, 6; election of 1852 and, 48; election of 1860 and, 68–70; eulogies of, as Lincoln's peer, 99–100; and Fourierism, 16–17; as Grant supporter, 96; in Harrison's presidential campaign, 20–21; and Johnson, 93–94; legacy of, 101–2; on Lincoln, 37, 95–96; and Lincoln eulogies, 91–92; as Lincoln opponent, 72, 84; and Lincoln's Cooper Union address, 59–60; Lincoln's correspondence with, 31, 86–87, *gallery*; Lincoln's life as interpreted by, 94; Lincoln's shared beliefs, 3; as Lincoln supporter, 84–85; memorial statue dedication, 100; Mexican-American War opposition, 32; and New York politics, 21–22; and *New York Tribune*, 5; peacemaking efforts with Confederacy, 83, 84–88; popular sovereignty position, 40; presidential appointments sought by, 71, 91; presidential bid, 96–98; and protectionism, 47; quotes attributed to, 44, 111; reforms favored by, 4; regard of contemporaries, 58, 108; and Republican Party, 49, 51, 56, 61–62, 64–65; senatorial bid, 72, 94–95; as slavery opponent, 11–13, 15, 35–37, 79–80, 82; Smithsonian Institute lecture, 75–76; as Taylor supporter, 33–34; in "The Slaughter of Seward" cartoon, *gallery*; travel from New York to San Francisco, 44–45; in *Vanity Fair* cartoon, *gallery*; Whig Party and, 23, 38; working class sympathies of, 15–16. See also *New York Tribune* (newspaper)

Greeley, Mary "Molly" Cheney, 16, 98
Greeley, Mary Woodburn, 15
Greeley, Zaccheus, 15

Hale, John P., 48
Hamilton, Alexander, 9
Hamlin, Hannibal, 65
Hanks, John, 62–63
Harding, Warren G., 101
Harpers Ferry raid, 58–59
Harper's Weekly (periodical), 98
Harris, Ira, 72
Harrison, William Henry, 14, 18–20, 22, *gallery*
Herndon, William, 29, 46, 63
Homestead Act, 24, 34, 37
Horace Greeley: Champion of American Freedom (Williams), 107
Horace Greeley: Nineteenth-Century Crusader (Van Deusen), 107
"House Divided" speech, 57

Illinois, legal climate in 1840s, 46
Indiana delegation, at Republican national convention, 65
infrastructure improvements, proposed, 2, 11

Jackson, Andrew, 7, 10–11, 16
Jackson, David S., 33
Jefferson, Thomas, and First Party System, 9
Jeffersonian (periodical), 17–18
Jewett, William Cornell, 83, 85
Johnson, Andrew, 93
Judd, Norman, 65

Kansas, proslavery and antislavery confrontations, 53
Kansas-Nebraska Act, 43, 49–50
Kaplan, Fred, 106–7
Knox, William, 46

Lamon, Ward Hill, 91
"Last Rail Split by 'Honest Old Abe'" (*Wide Awake Pictorial*), *gallery*

Lawrence, Kansas, sacking of, 53
Lecompton Constitution, 55
Lee, Robert E., 80–82, 90
legends, falsehoods in, 110–11
Liberal Republican Party, 96–97
Liberty Party, 25–26
Lincoln (Donald), 110
Lincoln, Abraham: in 30th Congress, 27; ancestors of, 5–6; assassination of, 91; autobiographical sketch for Scripps, 67; Chticago River and Harbor Convention, 1–2; Clay's eulogy, 42–43; Clay's presidential bid and, 24, 26; as congressman-elect from Illinois, *gallery*; Cooper Union address, 58–59; debates with Douglas, 9, 19, 53–55; education of, 6; elected president, 70, 90–91; elected to U.S. House of Representatives, 29; Frémont's electoral loss and, 52; on Greeley, 87–88; Greeley, correspondence with, 31, 74–75, 86–87, *gallery*; Greeley on, 82; to Greeley on peacemaking efforts, 85–86; and Greeley's editorial "Prayer of Twenty Millions," 78–79; Greeley's shared beliefs, 3; Greeley's support for, 45–46; on Greeley's support for Douglas, 56–57; on Greeley's wish for cabinet appointment, 71; Harrison's presidential campaign and, 19; "House Divided" speech, 57; and infrastructure improvements, 11; Kansas-Nebraska Act and, 43, 49; "Last Rail Split by 'Honest Old Abe'" cartoon, *gallery*; legacy of, 100–102; legal career, 27–28; marriage to Mary Todd, 8; martyrdom, 91–93; Mexican-American War criticism, 30–31; and the *New York Herald*, 88; Peoria speech, 49–50; personal tragedies during Civil War, 89; political career, 8–9, 28, 50; popular sovereignty position, 40; presidential campaign of, 45,
67–68; reading matter of, 46; regard of contemporaries, 108; response to perception as "Black Republican," 56; secession, fight against, 73; in "The Slaughter of Seward" cartoon, *gallery*; slavery, changing stance on, 11–12, 35–37, 49–51, 76–77; slavery, in debates with Douglas, 53–55; slavery in autobiographical sketch, 67; at Soldiers' National Cemetery dedication ceremonies, *gallery*; supporters of, at Republican national convention, 61–63, 64–65; Taylor's eulogy, 41; as Taylor supporter, 33; on Texas boundary, 31; in *Vanity Fair* cartoon, *gallery*; Whig Party and, 5, 14, 18, 20, 23; writ of habeas corpus suspended by, 76, 109; Young Men's Lyceum address, 11–12
Lincoln, Mary, 8, 91
Lincoln, Robert, 8, 27–28
Lincoln, Samuel, 5–6
Lincoln, Thomas, 13–14
Lincoln-Douglas debates, 9, 19, 53–55
Lincoln Memorial dedication, 101
Lincoln's Melancholy (Shenk), 110
Lincoln: The Biography of a Writer (Kaplan), 106–7
Lincoln the President (Randall and Current), 109
Logan, Stephen Trigg, 35, 63
Logan Act, 87–88
Log Cabin (newspaper), 15, 18, 21, *gallery*
London Daily News, 93
Louisville Journal (periodical), 14
Lovejoy, Elijah Parish, 11–12

Manassas battle (First Battle of Bull Run), 74
Matteson, Joel Aldrich, 50
McAdoo, William G., 100
McClellan, George B., 79–80, 84
Medill, Joseph, 28, 55, 60
Mexican-American War, 3, 12–13, 27, 29–33, 67

Missouri Compromise, 43
Montgomery Mail (newspaper), 58
Morgan, Matt, 98
Morning Post (newspaper), 16
Morning Star (London newspaper), 93
Morse, Samuel F. B., 23
"Mortality" (Knox), 46
mythology surrounding Lincoln and
    Greeley, 111–12

Nast, Thomas, 98
National Intelligencer (periodical),
    78–79
nationalism, in the American Sys-
    tem, 11, 26
National Republican Party, 6
"Nation's War-Cry" (*New York Tri-
    bune*), 73–74
nativist movement, 47
natural rights, 11
Neeley, Mark E., 109–10
New-Yorker (periodical), 16
New York Herald (newspaper), 81,
    88, 93
New York politics, 21–22, 61, 63–64
New York Times (newspaper), 65–66,
    81, 88
New York Tribune (newspaper): on
    Battle of Gettysburg, 81–82;
    Brisbane's column, 16–17; on
    Brown's raid and execution, 58;
    citizen journalism in, 108; course
    changes by, 73–76; editorial staff
    of, *gallery*; on end of war, 90; on
    fighting in Kansas, 53; Margaret
    Fuller and, 22; Greeley's presi-
    dential bid and, 97; Lincoln and,
    31; on Lincoln's assassination, 91;
    Lincoln's biography, 15; on Lin-
    coln's candidacy, 68; Lincoln's
    Cooper Union address in, 60;
    Lincoln's reelection bid endorsed
    by, 85; on Mexican-American
    War, 32; "Nation's War-Cry"
    column, 73–74; origins and
    approach, 21–22; promotion
    of dissident movement within
    Republican Party, 96; and pro-

tectionism, 47; publication of
    Sherman's battle plans, 76. *See
    also* Greeley, Horace
New York World (newspaper), 92
Niagara meetings, 83–89
Nicolay, John G., 75
Northern Spectator (periodical), 15–16
notes on sources, 105–13

Oglesby, Richard J., 62–63
Old Soldier (periodical), 19–20
Oregon delegation, at Republican
    national convention, Chicago, 61
*Overland Journey from New York to
    San Francisco, An* (Greeley), 44

panics: of 1819, 15; of 1837, 16; of
    1857, 53
Parker, Theodore, 58
partisan rhetoric in Lincoln-Douglas
    debates, 54
Parton, James, 98–99
party systems, 9–10, 45
Pennsylvania politics, 63–64
penny press, 16, 18
personal journalism, 78
Philadelphia Public Ledger (newspa-
    per), 51
philosophical perspective on life,
    nineteenth-century, 6
Pierce, Franklin, 48
"Plan of Adjustment" (Greeley), 85
Poe, Edgar Allan, 46
political alliances, in nineteenth
    century, 24
political communications, 23, 79
political debates, in small town
    culture, 54. *See also* Lincoln-
    Douglas debates
political party systems, 9–10, 45
political sensibilities, changes in,
    46–47
Political Text-Book for 1860 (Greeley),
    69–70
Polk, James K.: Chicago River and
    Harbor Convention, 1; as Demo-
    cratic presidential candidate, 25;
    and Mexican-American War,

Polk, James K. (*continued*)
12–13, 27, 30–32; and problems within Democratic Party, 38
popular sovereignty, 40, 48, 54
Pottawatomie Massacre, 53
"Prayer of Twenty Millions" (Greeley), 78
presidential campaigns: in 1860 election, 68–69; campaign slogans, 20; innovations in, 10, 18–19; press involvement in, 17
press, the: following the Civil War, 88; issues addressed before and after the war, 96; and Lincoln's assassination, 92–93; modern practices used in *Log Cabin*, 21; penny, 16, 18; in political campaigns, 17. *See also names of specific periodicals*
protective tariff issue, 24–25, 47

racist notions of Lincoln and Greeley, 13
Randall, James G., 109
Ray, Charles Henry, 28, 60
Raymond, Henry J.: advance in Whig circles, 52; advice to Lincoln, 73; on Battle of Gettysburg, 81; and Lincoln's Cooper Union address, 59; and Lincoln's reelection, 88; with *New York Tribune* editorial staff, *gallery*; on publication of letters between Lincoln and Greeley, 87; at Republican national meeting, Pittsburgh, 51; response to Seward's defeat, 65; in *Vanity Fair* cartoon, *gallery*
Recollections of a Busy Life (Greeley), 95
Reconstruction, 96, 99
Redpath, James, 53
Reid, Whitelaw, 98
Republicans and Republican Party: careers of Lincoln and Greeley and, 45; dissident movement within, promoted by *New York Tribune*, 96; Douglas and, 55; emergence of, 49; Greeley's

strategy for victory in 1860 presidential election, 56; Jefferson's vision for the United States and, 9; Lincoln's efforts to advance the party, 50; national convention, Chicago, 61–65, *gallery*; national meeting, first, at Pittsburgh, 51; response to Frémont's electoral loss, 52–53
Rhett, Robert Barnwell, 58
Ripley, George, *gallery*

Sangamon Journal (periodical), 14, 29
Schurz, Carl, 96
Scott, Winfield, 41, 47
Scripps, John Locke, 67, 107
secession, 72–73
Second Confiscation Act, 77, 78
Second Party System, 9–10
self-improvement concept, 7
self-made men, 3, 5–26, 115n. 5, 115n. 7
Seward, William H.: Emancipation Proclamation, preliminary, and, 77–78; and Greeley, 18, 21, 71, 87–88; gubernatorial campaign, 17–18; on "Higher Law" forbidding slavery, 51; "Irrepressible Conflict" speech, 57; loss of presidential nomination and support for Lincoln, 66; and New York politics, 21–22; popular sovereignty position, 40; as secretary of state, 72; in "The Slaughter of Seward" cartoon, *gallery*; supporters of, at Republican national convention, 62; in *Vanity Fair* cartoon, *gallery*; Weed's promotion of, for Senate, 33; Wood and, 65
Shakespeare, 46
Sharpsburg battle (Battle of Antietam), 79–80
Shenk, Joshua Wolf, 110
Sherman, William Tecumseh, 84, 90
"Slaughter of Seward, The" cartoon (*Cleveland Plain Dealer*), *gallery*
slavery: the American System and, 26; Clay's stance on, 11, 25, 42;

in Democratic peace platform, 84; as economic vs. racial issue, 13; Emancipation Proclamation, 77–80; end of, 80; Greeley's opposition to, 11–13, 15, 32–33, 35–37, 39, 78–80, 82; Harrison's position on, 18; in Lincoln-Douglas debates, 53–55; Lincoln on wrongs of, 76; in Lincoln's autobiographical sketch for Scripps, 67; Lincoln's changing stance on, 11–12, 35–37, 49–51, 77; Mexican-American War and, 32; Seward's denunciation of, 33, 51; telegraph introduction and issue of, 23; Whig party split over, 47

Snow, George M., *gallery*

social issues, regional, and the telegraph, 23

Soldiers' National Cemetery dedication, Gettysburg, *gallery*

Soule, John, 111

sources, notes on, 105–13

Speed, Joshua, 50–51

Spot Resolutions, 30, 37

Stanton, Edwin M., 78

Story, Francis V., 16

Stowe, Harriet Beecher, 99

Stuart, John T., 20

Sumner, Charles, 96

Swett, Leonard, 63

Taylor, Bayard, *gallery*

Taylor, Zachary, 31, 33, 38–40

Tecumseh, 20

telegraph, introduction of, 23

Texas annexation issue, 25

Third Party System of American politics, 45

Thirtieth Congress, 5, 27

Todd, Mary, 8, 91

Trumbull, Lyman, 50, 96

Tuscaloosa Independent Monitor (periodical), 25

Tyler, John, 20

Van Buren, Martin, 2, 10, 14, 17, 25, 39

Van Deusen, Glyndon G., 107

Vanity Fair (periodical) cartoon, *gallery*

Vauxhall Garden, 33

violence, proslavery and antislavery, 11–12, 53, 58–59

voter participation, 10

Warren, Fitz-Henry, 74

Washington, D.C., ban on slavery in, 77

Webb, James Watson, *gallery*

Webster, Daniel, 41

Weed, Thurlow: Chicago River and Harbor convention, 2; Greeley and, 17–18, 21; and New York politics, 21–22; popular sovereignty position, 40; Seward and, 51, 60, 65, 72; in "The Slaughter of Seward" cartoon, *gallery*; support for Taylor, 33

Welles, Gideon, 77

Wentworth, John, 57, 64

Whigs and Whig Party: antiwar sentiment, 29–33; attracting new voters, 39; divisions within, 25, 38; emergence following collapse of National Republican Party, 6–7; Illinois state convention, 18; Jefferson's vision for the United States and, 9; Lincoln-Greeley intersection, 5; Lincoln on idealism of, 23; national conventions, 18, 47; Panic of 1837 and, 16; regional priorities, 28–29; revolutionary political campaigns, 17; self-improvement concept, 7; Taylor's death and, 40–41, 47; vision of history, 6; voting rights position, 14

White, Hugh L., 14

Why I Am a Whig (Greeley), 48

Williams, Robert C., 107

Wilmot Proviso, 32, 36–37, 77

Wood, Julius, 64–65

Woodburn, Mary, 15

Workingmen, 16

World War I, 100–101

Gregory A. Borchard, a professor of mass communication and journalism in the Hank Greenspun School of Journalism and Media Studies at the University of Nevada, Las Vegas, is the author of *A Narrative History of the American Press*. He is a coauthor of *Lincoln Mediated: The President and the Press through Nineteenth-Century Media* and *The Press in the Civil War Era*. He is the editor of *Journalism History*, a journal published by the history division of the Association for Education in Journalism and Mass Communication, and he has produced a variety of monographs and journal articles that focus on the history of journalism and communication.

CONCISE
LINCOLN
LIBRARY

This series of concise books fills a need for short studies of the life, times, and legacy of President Abraham Lincoln. Each book gives readers the opportunity to quickly achieve basic knowledge of a Lincoln-related topic. These books bring fresh perspectives to well-known topics, investigate previously overlooked subjects, and explore in greater depth topics that have not yet received book-length treatment. For a complete list of current and forthcoming titles, see www.conciselincolnlibrary.com.

Other Books in the Concise Lincoln Library

Abraham Lincoln and Horace Greeley
Gregory A. Borchard

Lincoln and the Civil War
Michael Burlingame

Lincoln's Sense of Humor
Richard Carwardine

Lincoln and the Constitution
Brian R. Dirck

Lincoln in Indiana
Brian R. Dirck

Lincoln and the Election of 1860
Michael S. Green

Lincoln and Congress
William C. Harris

Lincoln and the Union Governors
William C. Harris

Lincoln and the Abolitionists
Stanley Harrold

Lincoln's Campaign Biographies
Thomas A. Horrocks

Lincoln in the Illinois Legislature
Ron J. Keller

Lincoln and the Military
John F. Marszalek

Lincoln and Emancipation
Edna Greene Medford

Lincoln and Reconstruction
John C. Rodrigue

Lincoln and the Thirteenth Amendment
Christian G. Samito

Lincoln and Medicine
Glenna R. Schroeder-Lein

Lincoln and the Immigrant
Jason H. Silverman

Lincoln and the U.S. Colored Troops
John David Smith

Lincoln's Assassination
Edward Steers, Jr.

Lincoln and Race
Richard Striner

Lincoln and Religion
Ferenc Morton Szasz with Margaret Connell Szasz

Lincoln and Natural Environment
James Tackach

Lincoln and the War's End
John C. Waugh

Lincoln as Hero
Frank J. Williams

Abraham and Mary Lincoln
Kenneth J. Winkle